T0104563

The
Graduate
Handbook

You Don't Know What You Don't Know

Russell J. Bunio

Order this book online at www.trafford.com
or email orders@trafford.com

Most Trafford titles are also available at major online book retailers.

© Copyright 2015 Russell J. Bunio.
All rights reserved. No part of this publication may be reproduced, stored in a retrieval
system, or transmitted, in any form or by any means, electronic, mechanical, photocopying,
recording, or otherwise, without the written prior permission of the author.

Print information available on the last page.

ISBN: 978-1-4907-6221-0 (sc)
ISBN: 978-1-4907-6220-3 (hc)
ISBN: 978-1-4907-6219-7 (e)

Library of Congress Control Number: 2015911022

Because of the dynamic nature of the Internet, any web addresses or links contained in
this book may have changed since publication and may no longer be valid. The views
expressed in this work are solely those of the author and do not necessarily reflect the
views of the publisher, and the publisher hereby disclaims any responsibility for them.

Any people depicted in stock imagery provided by Thinkstock are models,
and such images are being used for illustrative purposes only.
Certain stock imagery © Thinkstock.

Trafford rev. 12/29/2015

www.trafford.com
North America & international
toll-free: 1 888 232 4444 (USA & Canada)
fax: 812 355 4082

ABOUT THE BOOK, OVERVIEW

The Graduate Handbook: You Don't Know What You Don't Know was written in response to a number of questions asked of me by my nephew, soon to be off to college. Those questions revolved around careers, college majors, and being successful.

This book attempts to provide graduates with proven best practices that will help them when they enter the day-to-day workforce. Most sources of the best practices are from the many successful bosses I was fortunate to work for. Also, some of the sources are people who worked for me, students, and some work associates I worked with along the way.

I was a sponge.

I watched these people, I listened to them, and I learned those practices that I felt would help me perform my job. I cherry-picked their best methods and, in many cases, modified and tweaked those practices and made them my own. I practiced them and improved them through the years.

This is a handbook that helps new workers by telling them what they should do in building their career-starting foundation. The fifty best practices are short and to the point. They are a quick read and will hold the attention of the reader. They are not philosophical; they are practical.

In the book I use *workers*, not *employees*. That is intentional. I want the graduate to recognize the importance of what they are there to do—work!

My subtitle of the book, *You Don't Know What You Don't Know*, characterizes many young people as they go off to that first real job—eight hours a day, five days a week, or even more. This book will greatly improve the speed by which the graduate learns the basics. As an example, practice 1: always be early and leave late sets the stage for basics that ultimately lead to more complex practices—i.e. practice 47: compartmentalization.

Even though this book's user-customer is the graduate, the target sales customers are those parents, aunts, uncles, grandparents, friends, and relatives who are looking for something to buy for the upcoming graduate.(*) Graduation gifts are often difficult to select. Many relatives give money.

A gift of *The Graduate Handbook* <u>and</u> some money provide the graduate with something special. That special gift is fifty best practices that, if consistently used, will provide a jump start for the new worker.

Those sales customers that have read some of the practices say, "Wow, these are common sense. I wish I had known many of them when I started."

Yes, *we don't know what we don't know*!

*100% of the net proceeds from the sale of *The Graduate Handbook* will go to not-for-profit organizations that help people enhance and advance their lives.

Contents

INTRODUCTION xv

SECTION ONE: THE START 1

EARLY IN, OUT LATE 3
LOOK GOOD, SMELL GOOD..5
HARDWORKING...7
FROM ME TO WE...10
CUSTOMER FOCUS 13
CLEAR JOB EXPECTATIONS 15
MENTORED 18
DIRFT: DOING IT RIGHT THE FIRST TIME...........................21
HAVING FUN...23
WRITE IT DOWN (RID)..25

SECTION TWO: BUILDING YOUR ROLE 27

SECRETS, GOSSIP, RUMORS...29
PROFESSIONAL COMMUNICATIONS 32
EAT, SLEEP, EXERCISE 36
RELIABLE, TRUSTWORTHY 38
QUALITY 41
TEAMS...43
HUSTLE 47
THAT INTERVIEW..49

SECTION THREE: FOCUS YOUR EFFORT 54

MULTITASKING VERSUS FOCUSED EFFORT.........................57
FOCUS, FOCUS, FOCUS 59
ATTENTION TO DETAIL...62
A PLACE FOR EVERYTHING, AND EVERYTHING IN ITS
PLACE 65

LOOK, LISTEN, LEARN 67
CLOSE THE LOOP 69
PPP: PREPARE, PRACTICE, PRESENT 73
ETHICS AND ETHICAL BEHAVIOR............................76
BUILDING RELATIONSHIPS......................................80
BE THE BEST 83

SECTION FOUR: MOVING FORWARD, STEPPING UP 86

MEETINGS! MEETINGS! MEETINGS! 89
UP CLOSE AND PERSONAL.......................................93
VOLUNTEER: BE A LEADER 95
THE BLACK HOLE 99
STEP-BY-STEP.. 101
PRACTICING CPI.. 103
MEASURE IT 106
THE FIVE WHYS 109
GIVE ME MORE 112

SECTION FIVE: THE BIGGER PICTURE 114

SAVING TO INVEST 116
WHAT'S YOUR PLAN? 118
SEQUENCING 121
MAKE VISUAL 124
MAKE ACCOMPLISHMENTS KNOWN 127
SUPPLIERS AS PARTNERS....................................... 129
THOSE BOSSES 132

SECTION SIX: THE NEXT LEVEL 138

CONTINUOUS IMPROVEMENT BEATS POSTPONED
PERFECTION 140
FACTS AND DATA WILL SET YOU FREE 143
COMPARTMENTALIZATION 146
CUSTOMERS RULE 149
PEOPLE MAKE THE DIFFERENCE 153
ATTITUDE FEEDS ALL.. 156

THE END IS REALLY THE BEGINNING 161

ACKNOWLEDGMENT 163
SOURCES OF BEST PRACTICES 165

To Donald Snydel, my great friend who personified success in so many ways.

(February 23, 1948-February 15, 2015)

"Russ Bunio's book is packed with wisdom and is an eminently practical and useful guide to success. Every graduate hopes to be mentored by the very best, and this book is a great start (It's a sometimes "gotcha"reminder for experienced adults, too. I made a few notes, myself). I enthusiastically recommend the book, and our children and grandchildren will be the first among many on my personal mailing list".

-**James Henderson**, former President and Chairman of Cummins Engine Company

"Students entering the workforce are interested in learning how to be successful in their first job. As educators, we often struggle with credibility issues. Russell J. Bunio provides that credibility in his new book, The Graduate Handbook. That is why I have decided to use this resource in some of the courses we offer at the University of Iowa."

-**David Baumgartner** Assistant Provost, University of Iowa

". . . . I most came to admire about Russ over the years of working with him was his ability to lead his bosses, peers, associates, and staff and especially the way he mentored young employees. This is a book to be read and reread by anyone wanting to become better at what he or she does, especially those graduates just beginning to enter the work place."

-**Mark Chesnut** former Vice President of Human Resources, Cummins Engine Co.

. . . . "this book is based on several of his (Mr. Bunio's) successful real life experiences in working his way up from "worker" to a very high level "worker". I personally witnessed Russ's transformation from an old school management environment to leading a renaissance of enlightened management change at every organization he 'worked'in.

-**Carl Code** former Director of Materials Management-GM

"Mr Bunio is one of the most experienced management professionals I know. He shares his experience and knowledge through 50 best practices, which provide a foundation for young workers. When I read the book I was thinking I could do better if I read this kind of handbook when I graduated. Thank you for giving graduates a wonderful and useful handbook.

-Ren Bing Bing Vice President of Weichai Power, Ltd., General Manager of Linde Hydraulics Co. (China)

"This book should be mandatory reading for all new graduates or built into the on-boarding processes by the companies that hire them.

-Dr. Daren Otten Dean, Applied Academics Yuba College

"If I had The Graduate Handbook when I started coaching, I would not have made so many unnecessary mistakes. Every young college graduate should use The Graduate Handbook as a Business/Career Bible."

-Boots Donnelly former Middle Tennessee Head Football Coach and inductee into the College Football Hall of Fame (2013), and Tennessee Sports Hall of Fame (1997)

"50 Suggestions, 50 Good Habits, 50 Friends . . . .
The first time I open it (The Graduate Handbook), I regard it as a handbook for new workers. Then I figure out this book absolutely suit for almost everyone. No matter you are a new worker of a multi-billion dollar company, or a graduate of world famous university, you will find something useful".

-Saiyu Ren recent graduate (23 years old) from the University of New South Wales, Australia.

INTRODUCTION

Why Did I Write This Book?

Through the years I have been very fortunate to work for, and work with, some very successful people. You might say they are very smart, well educated, hardworking, or just lucky or maybe some combination of all. Anyway, by most standards these professionals are very successful in their fields, and at one time, they, like you, were just graduates starting out.

One of my nephews asked me years ago, "Uncle Russ, I want to be like you. What do I need to do?"
Somewhat surprised, I smiled, laughed, and asked, "What do you mean like me?"
"I want to make a lot of money," he responded without hesitation.
I smiled and then wondered, *Is he serious?*
His question made me reflect on this: how do we measure success, what is really important, and most importantly, how do I respond to his question? What advice can I give to a young person who is entering the day-by-day work environment? What have I learned, who have I learned the most from, and what advice can I give?
After some serious thought, I began to document what I learned. This book is about advice; you can take it, apply it, adapt it, and/ or ignore it. But it is advice based on *best practices* that work! These practices have worked for very successful people and have helped me along the way. Some of these practices you may already know about; others, not. The key is implementation, discipline, and making them part of your work ethic.

What Is Success (Money, Fame, Power, Happiness, Etc.)?

There is no one definition of *success*. The dictionary defines it as "something that ensures: the degree or measure of attaining a desired end."
There are several attempts to define success:

* Success is a dream come true after hard work.
* Success is to be rich and happy versus poor and happy—but the key word is *happy*.
* Success is reaching a place where your dreams were pointing to.
* Success is when you triumph over obstacles, barriers, and adverse situations.
* Success is a changing target or goal; it changes with time and conditions.
* Success is when you attain that which you sought.

Maybe success is a combination of these and other definitions; however, *you define success for you*. Many studies show that the successful person is generally characterized as happy, challenged, energized, focused, passionate, and persistent about his work.

Press on! Nothing in the world can take the place of persistence.
Talent will not; nothing is more common
than unsuccessful men with talent.
Genius will not; unrewarded genius is almost a proverb.
Education will not; the world is full of educated derelicts.
Persistence and determination alone are omnipotent.

—President Calvin Coolidge

Matching these attributes with *your* goals, aspirations, and dreams will make you successful. However, the end result, success, is defined by *you*.

What Are Best Practices? How Can They Help You?

Best practices
1) are a set of guidelines, ethics, and ideas that represent the most efficient or prudent course of action;
2) are methods or techniques that have consistently shown results superior to those achieved with other means; and
3) can be a baseline for continuous improvement, when you can better the best practice.

Key words here are *methods, ethics, techniques, guidelines, action, efficiency,* and *continuous improvement.* This book is about these and more.

Some may argue, what the best practice is for you may not be the best in the world. That is true. We don't have the ability to search the globe and compare the best to the better to the just good. The best is continuously moving and improving. Through benchmarking we are able to narrow that gap and continually drive closer and closer to the *best.*

What Is Benchmarking and How Does that Help?

Benchmarking is a quality tool that is a comparison of one organization's (or person's) best practices and performance against those of other organizations' (or persons').
Benchmarking seeks to identify standards, or best practices, to apply in measuring and improving performance.

When you benchmark, you document how you do something and then compare how others (usually someone that is noted for exceptional performance) do exactly the same process. You identify the differences and analyze the results (measurements).
If their process is superior to yours and the measured results are also better, then you may adopt or adapt to their approach.
Adopting or adapting those improvements to your process helps you improve and may lead to your creating a new best practice.

(Note: Benchmarking allows you to learn or confirm. You may learn something new that you can apply to your process. You are continuously improving. Or you may confirm you are doing the same or better than the benchmarked person or organization. You know you are on the right track, and now you have confirmed it.)

Where Do *The Graduate*'s Best Practices and Benchmarks Come From?

I have to admit, I did not create all the best practices in this book. Mostly I learned them; I sponged or borrowed them, modified them, and in some cases, improved the practices! Many successful people (I mentioned earlier) are the real creators of this book. I watched them in action, learned from them, and documented what they did to be successful and then tried to apply those practices to my work. Yes, I was a *sponge*.

At the end of this book, I listed many from whom I sponged, and I thank them for allowing me to do so, whether they knew what I was doing or not!

The Book's Customer

You, the graduates, are the customers of the book. The book is written to help you as you enter the workforce, as you initiate your career. I believe that by your reading, adopting, and practicing the fifty practices, you will shorten your learning curve and have the opportunity to use what successful professionals have created and used. This book will give you a jump start, an advantage, in that new, competitive workplace.

You will find that many of the best practices do not really focus on how to do something. They do clearly explain *what* you need to do. As an example, in the best practice "early in, out late" I explain what the desired result is, *what* you should do—always be at work early and usually leave a little late.

There are many books and training sessions on time management, and *The Graduate* does not take the deep dive into the how. I often give examples, recommendations, and explanations that focus on the *what*.

Best Use of *The Graduate Handbook*

My target was to write each practice to be clear, concise and easy to understand and to be a fast read. The goal was one page per practice. As you will see, I failed. I was not able to hold the one pager due to what was required to explain the practice.

However, to get the most out of the book, I recommend you read one practice, think about it, and try it out. Watch and see how others respond to your usage. Watch and see how your boss reacts. And see how the practice helps you with your job.

Some of the best practices may already be part of you or your approach. That's great, and you have a head start.

Your consistent use and adoption of these best practices will be recognized and appreciated. A hit-and-miss use will not. Your boss, fellow workers, and others will value consistency.

As you work your way through the list, you'll find some practices easy to implement, some more difficult. That's okay. Just remember, these practices came from very successful people, and I am sure their use did not always come easily or automatically.

What This Book Is Not, What It Is

This book is not a *how-to* book. It is not a *Dummies*, made-easy-type publication.

It is not a substitute for family, school, church, or other sources of learning. It is not an *end* that will allow you to be successful.

This book is a what-needs-to-be-done by a new person entering the workforce.

I hope this book will be one tool in your tool kit.

I expect it will be a *means* to your *end*.

That *end* is for you to be *successful*!

SECTION ONE: THE START

* Early In, Out Late
It does matter how much time you spend at work and when you come and go.

* Look Good and Smell Good
Your appearance makes an impression, no matter what job you do. Impressions do stick.

* Hardworking
Is there a difference between hardworking, working hard, or working smart?

* From Me to We
Your focus has to and will change.

* Customer Focus
Who is really your primary customer?

* Clear Job Expectations
You need them—understand them and excel at them.

* Mentored
It really helps to have a buddy, one who shows you the way!

* Do It Right the First Time
Being slow and correct beats being fast and wrong.

* Having Fun
Just because it is work, doesn't mean it cannot be fun.

* Write It Down
Remembering is good, forgetting is dangerous. Reduce stress and errors.

1

This is the only country in the world where today's employee is tomorrow's employer.

—Marco Rubio

The first day, week, and month of an employee's experience carries a lasting impression.

—Scott Weiss

The difference between who you are and who you want to be is the work you put in.

—Author Unknown

EARLY IN, OUT LATE

Some people are *always late*. Late for meetings, late for work, late for dinner, the movies, etc.

Even with activities that are very important to them, they seem to struggle to be on time. Being late is a serious problem when others rely on you, especially in a work environment.

Then at the end of the day, some workers practically *fly* out of work at the precise quitting time. Five o'clock comes and they storm out the gate.

Don't dare get in their way, or you'll be run over. There is something wrong with this approach, being late and exiting right on time every day.

Background

There have been many studies done and books written on effective *time management.* Why are some people always late? What is the root cause of habitual lateness? Those having this problem find the problem often revolves around their identifying actions to be done, setting priorities for those actions, and placing the priorities into sequence. Getting to work on time or early should be simple; you do this first, second, third, etc., etc., and allocate the appropriate amount of time to accomplish each. Stack the time requirements, add some contingency for unseen situations (i.e., heavy traffic) and a little extra time to be early, and the lateness problem should be remedied.

Being early every day is a major *plus*!

Your boss knows you are here, your co-workers know, and the day gets off to a good planned start.

Most work doesn't get completed on a set schedule. There will be times when it is for the best of the business or your coworkers that you make sure all is done and complete before leaving for the day. That magic five o'clock quitting time should be more of the wrap-up time than the quitting time. Take some time at the end of each day to review anything possibly missing completion for that day, as well as to prepare a list of major items to do for the next day.

Galen (my boss) said, "Watch Billy G. sometime. Watch the way he comes in and leaves. Bill is here every day usually about half an hour early—practically running through the gate to his work area. At the end of the day, he is dragging, walking slowly, and is always beyond normal quitting time. What does that tell you?"

Best Practice

The Billy G. example told me that *being early* helps everyone in the workplace and *leaving later* than quitting time shows dedication to the work. How you handle both ends of the workday will be noticed.

Notes

_____

_____

_____

_____

_____

_____

LOOK GOOD, SMELL GOOD

Often, there is no real simple answer as to appearance and dress for the new employee. Some companies or organizations have uniforms or dress codes.

Many organizations say just about anything is okay, but not jeans. Others say business casual is expected, but on Fridays they allow casual dress.

Some organizations say nothing. Maybe they expect nothing. Or when the employee gets out of the (undefined) box, the boss will say something to the employee. ("Your uniform is dirty, please get it cleaned and pressed!")

Background

Working in a factory—requires one type of dress
Working at a restaurant—requires another
Working outdoors—another
In an office—another

Some insightful observations:

* I once heard a senior VP say, "Here comes another one of those 'look good, smell good' guys—looks sharp."
This was the first impression made, and a very good one. Even without any mention of position or job performance, the new person was recognized in a very positive way.

* In our Mexico operation, it was recognized that the ladies working in the plant always looked like a million bucks (maybe pesos) even though they were working on the assembly line.
The job at the plant provided them work, but also a daily social opportunity. They wanted to, and did, look great. The guys also improved their appearance—wonder why?

* You don't know when the boss is going to call you into his office, to maybe meet his boss or a customer. This opportunity could come any day. That opportunity needs to be met by looking sharp.

* At the end of the day, George was tired—clothes were dirty, George was dirty, and he didn't smell so good. This was the nature of his job.
However, at the beginning of the next day, George was ready— clean George, clean clothes, and George smelled good.

* When Ernie came for the job interview, he wore a new suit, white shirt, sharp red tie, and his shoes were shined. He walked in with a smile on his face even though, I knew, he was very nervous. That first impression was exceptional, a very positive impression even before he spoke his very first word.

* Harriet once commented, "She dresses more like a boss every day even though she isn't—yet! All things being equal, she deserves and will get that next promotion."
And she did!

Best Practice
It is generally best to overdress than underdress in your work environment. Looking good and smelling good for your fellow workers, the boss, customers, and yourself helps prepare you for that next opportunity.

HARDWORKING

While the other guy's sleeping, I'm working. While the other guy is eating, I'm working. While the other guy's making love, I mean, I'm making love too, but I am working hard at it!
—Will Smith, (actor, producer, etc. etc.)

As you enter your new job, you will be asked to do things you've never done before. You can't expect to be able to do all of them well or 100 percent correctly. Your boss will understand that and will expect you to learn as you go. This is hard work.
This is part of the normal learning curve for a new employee.

Background

Often there is confusion between *hardworking*, *working hard*, and *working smart*.
* Being *hardworking* means you are focused, diligent, industrious, and you always put a lot of effort and care into your work. Your effort is directed to the completion of a task that you want to accomplish in order to meet your objective.

* *Working hard* often means doing a task that requires a lot or too much effort. The task is often described as backbreaking, laborious, unpleasant, hard, or tedious. Working hard often provides an opportunity for job improvement.

* *Working smart* is the result of using the best tools, technology, processes, and procedures that simplify the task and reduce the number of hours or physical energy required to complete that task.

You, as a new worker, will experience and travel through working hard, being hardworking, and working smart. Ultimately, through *kaizen*, working hard can diminish, allowing more time for being hardworking and working smart.

(*Kaizen* is a Japanese term, foundational to the Toyota production system, that means gradual unending improvement, doing little things better, setting—and achieving—ever-higher standards.)

Some Quotes of Note
* "Hard work beats talent when talent doesn't work hard." (Author Unknown)

* "What separates the talented individual from the successful one is a lot of hard work." (Stephen King)

* "I'm a great believer in luck, and I find the harder I work, the more I have of it." (Thomas Jefferson)

* "Nothing worth having comes easy." (Teddy Roosevelt)

* "All roads that lead to success have to pass through hard work boulevard at some point." (Eric Thomas)

* "Good things come to those who work their asses off and never give up." (Author Unknown)

Best Practice

The boss will understand that you will have to work hard as you learn the job. However, he will watch to see how you progress at working smart while showing him you're a hard worker. Hardworking employees are recognized and rewarded.

Notes

_____

_____

_____

_____

_____

_____

_____

_____

_____

_____

_____

_____

_____

FROM ME TO WE

Questions

* I am going to have to do what? You have to be kidding.
* I am so new, will I know what to say?
* What if I screw up and embarrass myself?
* I know I am the new member of the team, but why do I have to present for the entire team?
* Can't someone else with more experience do it?
* How will I know what to say, or worse, if someone asks me a question, what if I can't answer it?

Background

Most of us have belonged to a team, club, band, or some form of working-together group. In most cases, we volunteered to be on these groups because we wanted to participate and contribute in some way. We wanted to, so we did.

Now that you are entering the workforce, you will quickly see that wherever you work, you'll be pulled into a group or team where you will be expected to participate and contribute as a team member. The reason teams are so prevalent is that results obtained by teams are generally superior to results obtained by the individual. What I've seen is that teams will outperform individuals when...

1. the task is complex,
2. creativity is needed,
3. the path forward isn't clear,
4. more efficient use of resources is required,
5. fast learning is necessary,
6. high commitment is desirable,

7. cooperation is essential to implementation,
8. members have a stake in the outcome,
9. the task or process involved is cross-functional, and
10. no individual has sufficient knowledge to solve the problem.

A team is a group of people working together to achieve a common purpose for which they hold themselves mutually accountable. Team members sacrifice their individual objectives and goals to the betterment of the team's or group's objectives and goals. The transformation is from *me* to *we*!

In the list of *'Questions'*, you can readily see, that to the new team member, it is *I, I,* and *I.* "What if I, how can I, how will I . . . ?"

That is normal and expected. Especially as you start a new career, you want to do well, and being part of a team is part of the job, not the entire one.

Example, if you work in production, you have a functional responsibility to the production department. Your day-to-day job is focused on production. However, if there are quality problems in production, you will start to interface with quality, engineering, and maybe purchasing departments, to help work together to solve those quality problems. Working with this team and establishing what the team (*we*) can do to solve the problem subordinates the functional area (production) to the benefit of the team, in this case, to the business team.

Best Practice

Being part of a team is inevitable. Participating and contributing to that team will be expected. You're shifting from thinking and acting from a *me* to thinking and acting from a *we* is what teams are all about. *We* generate the best results.

Answers to the First Paragraph
Don't worry, we will all help you. We'll all help create your presentation, and we'll be there when you present. If someone asks a question you can't answer, one of us, we on the team, will answer for you. Don't worry, you won't screw up; we won't let you!
Notice all the we's!

Notes

_____

_____

_____

_____

_____

_____

_____

CUSTOMER FOCUS

As you start that new job, new career, you will find you have many customers. Who are they? What will they want? Are their expectations reasonable? Will you get to meet your customers? How will you satisfy those customers or, as others say *delight the customer*?

You will find, generally, there are two types of customers, direct and indirect.

Direct customers are those that you provide a product or service to and you have daily interaction with. You know what they need and want, and part of your job is to meet their expectations—daily, weekly, and monthly. Most of these customers are your coworkers, your bosses, and others.

Indirect customers are those who you may seldom meet or have direct interaction with. As an example, if you work at an IT company, you may seldom speak to an end user specifically about the finished product you helped produce.[1]

Background

Your first, direct, and primary customer is your boss! This is the person with whom you need to establish clear job expectations, make sure you know how the boss will evaluate your performance against job expectations, and how you can strive to meet or beat those expectations.

---

[1] One of your best experiences will come when you meet an end user, or customer. This is a great opportunity to see and hear what is important to the end user, how you may affect what is important. Getting into the shoes of the customer is very valuable!

The boss is in the position of trying to get multiple tasks done. Usually he (or she) has a number of workers assigned to him. Because of this scope of responsibility and authority, the boss will rely on his people to do their jobs.

Don't ever hesitate to ask questions—about the assignments, timing, and how to do the work. The boss expects this! When you fully understand your job expectations, the boss will feel more comfortable about your ability, your ability to meet those expectations.

The boss will rely on *you* to be there, be on time, and get your work assignments done.

If you cannot meet some of the job expectations, let the boss know, and know in advance when the deadlines are. Surprises are not good and should be kept to a minimum, especially when your performance may affect someone else's in the flow of services or products you produce. Others will rely on you, and if your performance *can* affect theirs, you must let them know and work with them to resolve the issues. You are now part of the production flow, an important part. You don't want to be let down, and neither will your coworkers!

Best Practice

You will have many customers. *Your primary customer is your boss!* Work closely with him, make sure you understand his expectations of you, and strive to meet or exceed those expectations.

CLEAR JOB EXPECTATIONS

How do you know when your job, task, assignment is complete? Have you done all that is expected of you? If all isn't done and you walk away, someone could be disappointed (90 percent complete isn't okay or acceptable).

Background

Everyone likes to get the job done, out of the way, finished. It feels good to complete something and then move on to something else that is more fun, more challenging, or as many graduates say, move on to something more creative.

Understanding what the task expectation is, is critical. Don't take anything for granted, and do go to your boss and say, "Please explain that to me again so I have it. I want to know what the expected finished product is."

You may get answers like this from your boss:

* You'll know when you're done.
* If you don't know by now, maybe you just don't get it.
* See me later, I'm busy.
* Talk to Mary—she'll show you what to do.
* Just do a quality job and you'll be okay. I'll let you know if it's wrong.
* Read the instructions, and if you have questions, see me.
* Just do it like the others do it.

Do any of these responses really help you? Some probably help, but will they allow you to actually *make sure* you do an excellent job? No!

The best approach is to go back to your boss and ask him to make very clear what is expected, AND what IS the time frame to get it done.

Sure, the boss is busy and has a lot going on; however, if there is a performance expectation, that expectation must be clear in your mind.

I once heard a new employee have this conversation with her boss:

Employee: "I'm not really sure of what I am doing. I don't want to disappoint you, but I am falling behind and will have a tough time catching up."

Boss: "Who else is on your team, can't they help you? I'm off to a meeting right now."

Employee: "Jim does a similar job, but he's so busy I can't get him to sit down for five minutes."

Boss: "Okay, I will be back in an hour, and let's walk through your questions and I'll answer them for you. Okay? For now, watch Jim and see what he's doing."

Employee: "Great. Thanks. Where do we meet and at what time?"

Boss: "At 1:00 p.m., at my office."

Employee: "See you there. Thank you"

Now this employee has the opportunity to be clear with the boss as to what the expectations and time frame are and maybe even how he will measure the performance.

The employee should walk into the meeting at 1:00 p.m. with a complete list of questions. If all the questions are answered and now the employee is clear, then the objective is met. If there is still uncertainty, then ask more questions until you are clear. Do take notes.

Job performance is extremely important, especially for new employees. Make every attempt to obtain what you need. Asking questions is not seen as a weakness; it is seen as a strength!

Best Practice

Having clear job expectations is critical to excellent performance. You must understand those expectations! By meeting or exceeding *agreed-to* job expectations, you will be successful.

Notes

_____

_____

_____

_____

_____

_____

_____

_____

_____

_____

_____

MENTORED

Welcome, you are now the new member of our team. We hope you enjoy your new job, and we all look forward to working with you. Let us know if there is anything you need, and we'll try to get it for you. Good luck to you!

Okay, now you are on the new job, and everyone seems nice, friendly, and helpful.
So when do we go for lunch? Where?
What time are breaks?
Can I have food in my cubicle?
Allowed to smoke anywhere?
What are the rules?
Who can answer all my questions?
These are normal questions running through the mind of any new person. How do you get these and many more questions answered? You shouldn't go to the boss for everything!

Background
The questions raised here are all normal questions for the new person. The best and simplest way to address this situation is to ask the boss, "Do we have a mentorship or buddy system in place to help new employees like me?"

Mentorship

A *mentor* is a person who provides guidance to a less-experienced employee. Often, the mentor is an experienced coworker who is well respected within the organization. Often called a buddy system, mentorship is a win-win. The employee benefits, as does the employer.

Benefits to person mentored. The mentor can:
1. Show how things work,
2. Help solve a problem,
3. Critique work,
4. Introduce others to the new person (reduce isolation),
5. Be an advisor, and lastly,
6. Show the ropes to the new person.

Benefits to the employer:

1. Greater employee productivity
2. Faster improvement on the job
3. Fewer mistakes made
4. Employee satisfaction generally better
5. Sure beats the sink-or-swim approach
6. Probably less employee turnover

Best Practice

As a new employee, you want to do a good job, grow on the job, and satisfy that primary customer—the boss. By asking if there is a mentorship program in place you are taking the initiative and showing your desire to do well.

If there is a program in place, great. If not, your boss may realize this is a good idea and implement one.

Ask to have a mentor.

Notes

_____

_____

_____

_____

_____

_____

_____

_____

_____

_____

_____

_____

DIRFT: DOING IT RIGHT THE FIRST TIME

We all make errors and mistakes, have misfires, and even commit blunders—only those who do nothing, make no mistakes. Even the most experienced sometimes don't get it right every time or the first time. Later in the quality best practice, the emphasis is on knowing what the requirements of quality are and then working to meet or exceed that requirement.

DIRFT goes hand in hand with this practice. Our goal is zero defects!

Background

Fixes, repairs, reworks, rejections all result in time lost and increased costs. Philip Crosby, a quality guru, had it right. The four major principles that support DIRFT are these:

1. The definition of quality is conformance to requirements (*requirements* meaning both the product and the customer's requirements).
2. The system of quality is prevention.
3. The quality standard is zero defects (relative to requirements).
4. The measurement of quality is the price of non-conformance.

The key concepts are *conformance* to requirements, *preventing* defects, non-conformance has a *price*, and the goal is *zero defects*.

It doesn't matter if you are making a product, providing a service, or creating a report for others; your goal is to do an excellent job, on time, with zero defects.

Easy to say, not always so easy to do.

What may cause you to *not* create that zero-defect quality product?

* Not having a clear understanding of the work assigned

* Rushing the work and trying to complete it without sufficient time
* Being unprepared
* Not having a focus on the work
* Leaving the work unfinished or half-done
* Taking shortcuts

Here is a list of steps that will help do it right the first time:

1. Spend the time and make sure you are clear as to what the assignment is and there is agreement on what the finished product should look like.
2. Allocate the necessary amount of time to get the project done in addition to 10 percent for overruns or unforeseen issues.
3. Focus on the project; eliminate distractions.
4. Check your work as you go. Quality checks through the process will save time in the end.
5. Be methodical and not in a hurry.
6. Quality-check your finished product. Are you meeting the assignment expectation? Are there any obvious errors such as spelling errors, typos, or slight blemishes?
7. Have someone else's fresh eyes take a look at the work or project—anything missed?

Best Practice

Striving for zero defects in what you do will be supported by the seven steps listed above. Doing it right the first time, resulting in zero defects, not only reduces costs, but also improves the quality of your product or service. Your customers expect that quality!

Do it right the first time; you may not get a second chance.
—Author Unknown

HAVING FUN

Just because you have started work or a new career doesn't mean that your workplace cannot be fun. You should have some fun, and creating that environment with coworkers can be both socially rewarding and very supportive of job accomplishment.

Background

Some will argue that working is work and there is no time for anything but doing your job. They believe the boss doesn't want you wasting time, goofing off, or just plain socializing much. Work hard and that's it. That's what you are being paid to do.

Others will say enjoying your work, positively interacting with coworkers, having some laughs as you do the work will make you more productive in the long run. These folks argue that job fulfillment is the most important criteria for job success.

In reality, both approaches have some merit.

Most bosses want their workers productive and happy.
They do know that the *most productive* workers are
* punctual,
* focused,
* motivated,
* enthusiastic,
* happy and enjoy their work, and
* like their bosses.

The Complainer
Did you ever work around someone who hates his job, complains about everything, and really has nothing positive to say? I can't imagine being faced with this attitude eight hours per day.

The Loafer

Have you worked with someone who just goofs off any chance he gets? He looks for ways to avoid work. His days are very long, as are yours, since you must work with him. At quitting time, he runs from the work area and says, "I'm outta here!"

The Performer

It is easy to identify the motivated worker, who is on the job early, leaves a bit late, focuses on the job at hand, and finds ways to enjoy the work and the work environment. He is easy to work with and is recognized for his good attitude and performance.

Best Bet

Come to work to get the job done (first) while having some fun (second)! Most coworkers will enjoy being around you as someone who does a good job and enjoys doing it. Set the example and others will follow. And the group's performance will be what the boss will be looking for.

Best Practice

Find ways to have fun at work so you enjoy the workday. If you can't find some form of fun in your job, maybe you better look for another opportunity!

Do it well, make it fun—the key to success in life, death, and almost everything in between.

—Ronald P. Culberson, author

WRITE IT DOWN (RID)

It probably isn't very fashionable today to actually write something down on paper or keep notes. How often do we hear someone say:

* Oh, sorry, I forgot that. (Or as some say, "My memory didn't serve me.")
* No problem, I'll remember to take care of that.
* I keep turning over in my mind something I don't want to forget. Can't sleep.
* What do I need? I don't have a list—oh well, just wing it.
* Where is that telephone number? Who said they were going to take care of that assignment?

Background

Writing something down really does save time, energy, and frustration. Using random scraps of paper or just relying on memory can be unreliable and dangerous. The more you are expected to do and remember, the better your system needs to be.

Here Are Some Effective Practices
Ted always carried a very small notebook (about three by three) in his pocket, and as things would come up, he would write them in the book, as his reminder items. That book was always with him. At the end of the day, he would look at the book to make sure he would remember everything. Today, Ted is a vice president at Toyota.

Charlie kept a list at his desk. As things that he couldn't take care of right at that time would come up, he would write them on his list of *to-dos*. During the day, Charlie would work from the list to make sure nothing of importance would be missed. At the end of the day, he would review the list before going home and prepare a priority list for the next day. His mind was clear, all was done, and a get-started list was ready for the morning.

Galen often would wake up during the night and be thinking, *I must remember to do this and that and that*. He would turn this over in his mind, over and over, for fear of forgetting it. Finally, Galen decided to place a pencil and paper near his nightstand so that if he would want to remember something, all he would have to do is write it down. He did this and his turning over and over stopped. His mind was at ease, and he didn't forget.

Best Practice

Don't always try to remember everything. It is very important to not forget, and the best way to avoid forgetting is to *write it down* and be *rid* of the worry of forgetting.

SECTION TWO: BUILDING YOUR ROLE

* Secrets, Gossip, Rumors
These are watch-outs! Sometimes it's just best to say nothing.

* Professional Communications
What you say, how you say it, and when to say it are all important.

* Eat, Sleep, Exercise
Make sure the right balance receives priority.

* Reliable, Trustworthy
You can become very valuable, leading to indispensable.

* Quality
Most think they know what quality is; few know how to clearly
define it. Here is a simple, easy definition for your use.

* Teams
Why teams deliver the best results and can help you move up.

* Hustle
Most believe it is better to do something versus nothing. Failure is
okay. Failure often provides a spring-board to success.

* That Interview
Here are four phases to follow to carry out a successful interview
(process).

Teamwork is the ability to work together toward a common vision. It is the . . . ability to direct individual accomplishment toward organizational objectives. It is the fuel that allows common people to attain uncommon results.

—Andrew Carnegie

Take care of your thoughts when you are alone. Take care of your words when you are with people.

—Unknown Author

Talent wins games, but teamwork and intelligence win championships.

—Michael Jordan

A boss promotes the reliable employee to higher positions, the professor offers research opportunities to the reliable student, (and) the team picks the reliable man as its captain.

—Brett and Kate McKay

SECRETS, GOSSIP, RUMORS

Is there such a thing as a secret in the workplace? When you hear someone say, "Can you keep a secret?" does that indicate that this person is passing a secret from another or just wants to confide in you?

Rumors, gossip, and so-called secrets are commonplace in most workplaces. We all want to know what is going on. We don't want to be left out in the cold. Or do we?

Background

Here are some safe guidelines to follow when being exposed to those rumors, gossip, and secrets:

Speaking

1. Treat secrets as not secrets—at best they are limited exposure of information to select people. If someone wants to tell you a secret, just say, "I'm really poor at keeping secrets, so if this is to be confidential, please don't tell me because I'm not so good keeping silent."

2. Gossip usually hurts people, not helps them. If you have something positive to say about someone, say it. If you are tempted to say a negative, just say nothing. Ask yourself, *Would I feel comfortable saying the gossip to the person's face, openly and honestly?* If you are, it is probably okay. If not, you should say nothing.

3. Rumors are like grass fires. They may start from a small spark, slowly spread, ignite more, and then rapidly burn out of control. Rumors can cause a lot of damage. Rumors can usually be dispelled by talking with your boss, checking your organization's policies, or sometimes just asking yourself, "Is this rumor too good, or too bad, to really be true?" And you know what, when it is *too good or too bad*, it is usually a bad rumor. Does that rumor pass the smell test?

Writing

1. By reducing something (a secret) to writing, you have become a partner in the secret-spreading flow. Now you will pass that non secret to others, and you are just as guilty as the secret's originator. Remember, you may be passing information that is bad, inaccurate, or just hurtful.

2. E-mails and social media are potential hotbeds for gossip and rumors. What you write can have your name attached to it forever. How you feel and think today will change. Relationships and friendships change, and you need to be cautious as to what you reduce to writing and share with

others. Over time, you may regret *publishing* so much for the world to see.

If in doubt, stop and think. *If what I am saying or writing would show up on the front page of my hometown newspaper, would my parents be proud of me or disappointed?*
If there is *any doubt* in your mind, don't do it!

Best Practice

There are no real secrets in the workplace; gossip should be avoided, and rumors are usually a waste of time and energy.

Notes

_____

_____

_____

_____

_____

_____

_____

_____

_____

_____

_____

PROFESSIONAL COMMUNICATIONS

Recently, while sitting next to a mother and daughter at a local restaurant (friends of our friends), I asked them where they were from (Tennessee) and what the daughter was up to other than being out to dinner at this restaurant. Smiling, the daughter replied, "I am a student at Colorado State University, and I am studying business and finance."
I asked, "What year are you?"
And she said, "I am a junior, *sir.*"
My wife then asked the young lady, "When you graduate, will you look for a job in Colorado, Tennessee, or here in Florida?"
She said, "*Ma'am*, I'm not sure, I do love my home state."

After other discussions around the table, I said to the young lady, "We do appreciate your *yes, ma'am* and *yes, sir.* It is refreshing!"
Again, smiling, she said, "Thank you, sir, but some of my friends at school make fun of me because I do say *sir* and *ma'am.* I can't help it. It's just the way I was brought up."

Our first impression of this young lady was very positive. *Yes, sir!*

Background

Every day we have many opportunities to communicate—face-to-face, text, e-mail, phone, letters, cards, and others. These opportunities are very important because they not only give us the vehicle to communicate content but also a vehicle to create an impression about ourselves.
Verbal and visual communication is generally accepted as the optimal opportunity for the most effective communication.

Here are some pointers:
One of my bosses would often say, "It's not so much about what you say, it's about how you say it. It's how you present yourself." How would you like it said to you? How do you get across the message so the other person listens and hears? Always try to be thoughtful, considerate, honest, and open. If you were on the receiving side, how would you want to hear the message?

Everyone likes to hear their name when being addressed. "Good morning, Jack! How are you, Kathy?" Looking at a person and saying "Have a great evening and see you tomorrow, Jan," will generally get a positive response back to you. A regular "hello" is always appreciated. Especially a "hello" with a name attached.

A common filler so often used is *like*. Some people will beat "like, like, like" to death and use the word to allow time to think or just fill in the blanks. This word and other repetitive words or phrases do become old very quickly. An easy way to stop their use is to slow down and think of other words to use in their place. Effective and professional communication is not a race. Slowing down and thinking about what you want to say will pay dividends.

Have you ever heard "It takes more muscles to frown than it does to smile"? I never confirmed that just because I never really checked it out. Whether it requires more or less muscles isn't the point. Smiles and laughter are contagious. Smiling at someone almost always gets you a smile in return. Laughing at yourself and with others creates a positive environment, an environment that others enjoy and want to be part of. A simple thing like smiling is an effective and positive form of communication.

Most everyone likes to talk and often talk about themselves. It is easy since they know about themselves and want to share with others what they are doing, what they think, or what others are doing that they know about. Being a good listener is sometimes difficult. It is hard to listen to someone ramble on and on. The challenge is to listen and then speak when it counts.
A good listener is rewarded with learning something (good or bad, fact or fiction) and can provide meaningful input (when he can get a word in edgewise).

Look 'em in the eyes! There is always time for tweeting, texting, and e-mailing. They have their time and place. When you have the opportunity to speak with someone face-to-face, take advantage of that opportunity. *Don't avoid it; embrace it!* Maintain eye contact through the discussion. This focused attention will be positively received.

When writing something, reread what you've written to make sure it says what you want (say what you mean and mean what you say). Lastly, are the grammar and spelling correct? Who knows where this document may end up. Make it clear and make it right!

Best Practice

These seven examples do add up to a best practice for professional, effective communication. Others do and will watch how well you communicate.

Notes

_____

_____

_____

_____

_____

_____

_____

_____

_____

_____

_____

EAT, SLEEP, EXERCISE

Advice from a father to his son about work, school, and being off on his own:

You need to eat well, three good meals a day—breakfast is very important. Don't forget about enough sleep, maybe seven to eight hours per day. And last, you need exercise every day—some exercise.

Sure sounds like what we've all heard before—just common sense.

Background

On one of my visits to China, I had an opportunity to sit with a family over dinner and meet their son (home for the holiday), who is a student and who works in the USA. The son puts a lot of pressure on himself to do well. He is very dedicated to his studies and his job. He wants very much to create a good impression, make friends, and become part of the university life. He knows that his family is very invested in his education, and he doesn't want to disappoint them in any way.
The father said, "The only advice I gave my son was to take care of himself and make time for his health, sleep, eat, and exercise."

There was no mention of don't do this or don't do that. He didn't say don't go to wild parties, don't drink or smoke. All the words were very positive, and there was real focus on "taking care of yourself."

We talked about how difficult it was for the son to live by these guidelines. The pressure of the school and job often conflicted with the three easy things to do. There are days when there is just not enough time to do all of what is expected. There is a lot of give and take.

The father said, "All else is important but not as important as keeping the body healthy and working. Your first job is to take care of yourself then take care of school and the job. Invest in your health just like you do in school and your job."

ENOUGH SLEEP

BALANCED DIET *DAILY EXERCISE*

Best Practice

It really sounds so simple—eat, sleep, exercise. Who doesn't know that these three activities are very important? Who tries to intentionally ignore them? However, it is so easy to take the shortcut and move them to the back of the line. I have often talked about what you might add to your tool kit. Your personal health is a must!

Notes

_____

_____

_____

_____

_____

_____

_____

_____

RELIABLE, TRUSTWORTHY

I do trust you. I want to trust you more and give you more responsibility. I can't do it all myself, and I want you to take on more each day.

—The Boss

Background

From a boss's perspective, *reliability* is the passageway to trust.

Reliability is:

* "The ability to be depended upon, as for accuracy, honesty, achievement".
* "When you take on responsibility for your actions . . . and deliver".
* "When employees are reliable, when they are punctual, do their work with a minimum of errors, and put the job first".
* "When a person does what he says he is going to do."

Reliability>>generates>>trust.

Real-Life Example
Ron and his team were responsible for providing paint to the paint line. Tonight the line was going to run short of paint, the line would shut down, and thirty people would be sent home early—with reduced pay.
No paint.
No work.
Not good!
Ron contacted the supplier and made expedited arrangements to fly the paint from the supplier to a local airport and have the paint picked up by a carrier. If all would go *as planned*, the paint would

arrive at the plant by 10:00 p.m. and the third shift of production would have the paint needed. Ron made all the necessary calls and connections with the paint supplier, their shipping department, the airfreight carrier, the trucking companies, the plant receiving inspection, and the production supervisor in the plant.

As Ron's boss left at 6:00 p.m., he asked Ron, "Are we okay on paint tonight, we going to get it?"

Ron said, "All is arranged, and I'll make sure it gets here."

The boss left.

Ron called the supplier again at six fifteen. "Is the paint ready?"

"Yes."

Ron talked with the carrier. "Are you on the way to get the paint?"

"Yes."

Half an hour later, to the carrier he asked, "Do you have the paint at the airport? The plane on time?"

"Yes."

He called the carrier at the arriving airport. "The plane arrived and you have the paint?"

"Yes."

"How long till you are at the plant?"

"One hour."

Ron, at nine, called the plant receiving inspection. "The paint arrived yet?"

"Yes, we're unloading it now."

At nine thirty, Ron called the production foreman. "You have the paint? All okay?"

"Yes, we have it, it's on the line and we're painting!"

Best Practice

Ron was reliable, and he had the trust of the boss to get it done. The reliable worker, one who does what he says he's going to do, develops trust with his boss, coworkers, suppliers, and customers. Reliability generates trust!

Notes

_____

_____

_____

_____

_____

_____

_____

_____

_____

_____

_____

_____

QUALITY

That car is sweet and has super quality. We all know the Japanese make the highest-quality cars. J. D. Power confirms this. What do I know about quality?

My boss says he wants me to do a quality job, whatever that means!

Quality is in the eye of the beholder.

Quality is job 1!

Quality always comes first, cost second.

Quality is expensive.

If you don't have quality, you don't have customers.

And a favorite, if you have quality, the customer comes back; if you don't, the product comes back—*your choice*.

Background

Everyone talks about quality and how important it is.

The dictionary defines it as "an essential or distinctive characteristic, property, or attribute; high grade, superiority, excellence; producing or providing products or services of quality or merit." Hundreds of books have been written about quality, quality principles, and quality practices. These writings go into excruciating detail about building quality, the cost of quality, and how to design processes to reach high standards of quality in products and services.

There are many, many gurus who have contributed to the development of quality principles and practices.

1. W. Edward Deming
2. Kaoru Ishikawa
3. Joseph M. Juran
4. Philip B. Crosby
5. Malcolm Baldrige
6. Others

So when someone says you need to do a *quality job*, what does that really mean? A job done quickly and on time? A job done with no errors? A finished product that looks good and lasts? A product that works and doesn't break down?

One of the easiest definitions to remember, and maybe the most inclusive definition, is by Philip Crosby, from the Quality College, Winter Park, Florida: "Quality is conformance to requirements."

If you know what the requirements are (specifications of the finished product—the what—and timing to get the product complete—the when) and you meet or exceed (conformance) these two clearly defined requirements, you are providing a quality product or service.

Best Practice

Spend the necessary time with your boss to clearly define what a *quality job* is. Knowing the specifications of the finished product and the timing for completion will definitely help you do a quality job.

It is to your benefit and your boss's benefit to reach agreement.

TEAMS

Most all of us have been on a team of one sort or another. We celebrate our wins and try to forget our losses. *Get 'em next time.* And then we move on.
We learn important skills in the process, such as teamwork, relying on others, sharing a common goal, performing our role, competition, the importance of practice, and on and on. Those excellent experiences will carry over into the workplace. However, the main reason for using teams in the workplace is that the use of teams are usually the smartest way to achieve a goal.

Background

Most of the teams we associated with were sports, clubs, bands, or volunteer associations. These experiences were very important in our development and often allowed us to compete with others similar in age or interest. We often volunteered or tried out to be able to participate on these teams. We felt good about making the team and being accepted.

When you enter the workforce and there are teams, you will become part of a performance-driven group effort (like it or not). You will be expected to pull your load, contribute to the success of the team, and help others in the process.

No one sits on the bench if they can't or don't perform. Most teams are small (maximize efficiency and maintain low costs) and are very focused on their goal, usually a goal that cannot be reached by an individual.

Here are some similarities and differences between *sports teams* and *work teams*:

Sports	Work
1. Common goal	1. Common goal
2. Requires practice for best results	2. Requires practice for best results
3. *Major recognition for stars*	3. *Recognition for each team member*
4. *Promotes structure and tolerates creativity*	4. *Promotes and seeks activity*
5. Recognize and utilize leaders	5. Recognize and utilizes leaders
6. *Practice is before the contest*	6. *Practice is during the contest*
7. *Plays the game once or twice a week*	7. *Performs the work each day*
8. *Receive trophies or certificates for winning*	8. *Receive compensation for excellent performance*
9. *Best teams win and move on*	9. *Best teams win and move up*

Why do businesses and work groups use teams? Teams often are seen to cost more money, require more people, and are slower in getting results.

So what is the big deal? What are the benefits of using teams in the workplace?

* Teams provide a wider range
  of ideas and suggestions to solve problems.
* Teams that work together motivate one
  another as they focus on the task at hand.
* Teams often can accomplish much more
  than an individual can.

* *No idea is a bad idea* comes to life on teams, and some of those "bad" ideas, when fully explored (and sometimes modified), end up being the right idea for the task.
* Some workers are cautious and risk averse; gaining support and consensus of others on a team sometimes drives home the risky and best solution.
* Most teams contain some form of diversity in backgrounds, experiences, and cultures. This diversity brings new ideas and generates open-minded discussion and open-minded solutions.
* Teams help workers identify leadership skills and leaders on the team.
* Since team members are reliant and dependent on one another, team members more quickly help other team members. Team member growth and development help all on the team.
* Teams may appear to be slower (meetings, consensus building, negotiations, etc., etc.), and they may be; however, the results are usually superior, of higher quality, and easier to obtain support for implementation.
* Being on a team is more fun, and success is shared and celebrated together.

Best Practice

In the workplace, when called upon or asked to join a team, *do it*!
Volunteer!
The work experience will allow you to continue your job growth.
Whether a team member or a team leader, you will learn and grow,
and that growth will make you more valuable to other workers, the
boss, and the organization.
Volunteer!

HUSTLE

Every morning in Africa, a gazelle wakes up. It knows it must run faster than the fastest lion, or it will be killed. Every morning a lion wakes up. It knows it must outrun the slowest gazelle, or it will starve to death. It doesn't matter whether you are a lion or a gazelle. When the sun comes up, you'd better be running.

—Author Unknown

Background

There are those who will think about *it*, procrastinate about *it*, and will not get it done. There are those who will talk a good game, but when the time comes to play, they don't. And of course, there are those who say and believe "I just can't find time to get it done" instead of making the time necessary to get it done.

Action,
speed,
aggressiveness,
accomplishment
are not apparent
in their work spirit!
Are they overly tentative?

Versus

Others embrace action and focus on getting *it* done and getting *it* behind them. When it is game time, they are suited up, ready to play, and are early onto the field. These workers make time, complete the task, and look for more to do.
Action, speed, aggressiveness, *hustle,* and accomplishment are in their work spirit.

47

These sayings are dated but somehow continue to live on with meaning:

* He who hesitates is lost!
* The early bird gets the worm.
* It's not the size of the dog in the fight; it's the size of the fight in the dog.
* Don't put off til tomorrow what you can do today.
* A bird in the hand is worth two in the bush (back to the birds?).

These sayings reinforce the desire to get things done, make progress, and not hesitate or delay.
Failure by doing nothing is failure by omission.
Failure by doing something is failure by commission.
Most bosses I know, fully understand failure but have much less patience with failure by omission. Doing something and failing can result in the positive.

* "I have not failed. I've just found 10,000 ways that won't work." (Thomas Edison)
* "Failure is simply the opportunity to begin again, this time more intelligently." (Henry Ford)
* "It's fine to celebrate success, but it is more important to heed the lessons of failure." (Bill Gates)
* "When I was young, I observed that 9 out of 10 things I did were failures, so I did 10 times more work." (George Bernard Shaw)

Best Practice

In the day to day work environment, bosses would rather slow you down versus push you when it comes to completing assignments.
By having an aggressive, hustled, get-stuff-done approach, you will get results (with some failures), and those results will be recognized and rewarded.
And when the sun comes up, you will be running!

THAT INTERVIEW

It's time for that job interview. "What do I say? What should I not say? What if I make a lot of mistakes and blow this chance? How do others get through this? Are there real secrets to having a good interview that gets me the job? I know I'll be nervous, and who wouldn't be? Anything I can do to stay cool?"

"I may get one shot at this, and I need and want this job!"

Background

Just about everyone can provide the interview candidate with ideas, and most are probably pretty sound recommendations based on some degree of experience. Most of us have been on both sides of the interview table and are aware of the stress an interview may place on a prospective employee. This stress and nervousness is taken into consideration by the interviewer, and generally, the interviewer will try to make the interviewee comfortable.

There are a number of phases that, if properly followed, will help you with a smooth, comfortable, successful interview.

* Phase 1: Preparation
* Phase 2: Practice
* Phase 3: Execution
* Phase 4: Follow Up

Preparation

It sounds simple (it generally is), but you need to do some homework.

Try to learn as much as you can about the organization, group, or company that you want to join. Search the Internet, talk with others who work for this organization, or visit the library (still a great source of information). Document what you learn and prepare a list of questions you might want to ask the interviewer.

Think about some questions that might be asked of you and prepare your answers, such as these:

* Do you have any travel restrictions?
* Are you willing to transfer out of the town, state, or country?
* Can you work any shift and overtime?
* Where do you want to be in five or ten years? What position?

(Positive answers are generally a good sign of flexibility.)

Think about the job for which you are being interviewed. What are the expectations of this job, and how would you meet them? Is the job just a job or the start of a career? Besides money, why do you want this job (career growth, opportunity, field of interest, others)? Is there any prereading material provided by the interviewer that should be read before the interview? If none is provided, you might ask the interviewer if there is, such as...

1. a job description;
2. work plans and/or appraisal forms, etc.; or
3. organization's philosophy, principles, mission statement, any policies.

Anything provided to you by the interviewer should be read and studied, and any questions should be listed for the upcoming interview.

Practice

Now is the time to focus on practicing for the interview. The more you practice, the better you'll get. You will probably have one-half to one hour for the interview, and the interviewer will ask most of the questions. There is no list of standard questions or standard interview approaches. The person who interviews you will want to get to know you, get to know you over and above what has been supplied in advance.

I find the best way to practice is to spend time with someone who can play the interviewer role with you (know anyone in HR or with a lot of experience?).

Have them ask you interview-type questions.

Have them listen to your responses and give you feedback.

Have them tell you what went well and what could be improved upon.

Also, spend some time thinking about that first impression you will make. Practice with your interviewer friend and do the following:

1. Smile.
2. Try to relax as best you can.
3. Maintain good eye contact.
4. Listen intently to the questions.
5. Think before you answer; speedy responses are not the priority.
6. Answer the questions honestly, and be concise.
7. Be aware of the "like, like, like" trap in communications; slow down to answer the questions.
8. Select what you will wear and what you'll take into the interview (notes binder, notebook, iPad?).
9. Ask those questions you might have for the interviewer, and listen to the answers.

Execution

This is what you have prepared for and practiced for. Here are some observations of successful interviews:

* The candidate was prepared and knew about the organization.
* The candidate appeared relaxed, answered all the questions, and smiled through most of the interview.
* The candidate has a positive attitude, a good appearance, and appeared to be comfortable and flexible as to assignments.
* The candidate asked good questions and took notes.
* The candidate came across as open, honest, friendly, and sincere.
* At the end of the interview, the candidate thanked the interviewer for spending the time with him, said he hoped he made a positive

impression to meet the job expectations, and firmly shook the interviewer's hand, accompanied by a smile and a sincere *thank-you.*

Follow Up

After the interview, and allowing some time to take a deep breath, go off somewhere and make some notes on how the interview went, from your perspective.

1. What went well?
2. What would you do differently had it not gone well? How better could you have prepared?
3. How better could you have practiced?
4. What should you do differently at the next job interview?
5. What questions did you have a hard time answering?

That day or the next, take the time to send the interviewer a note to say something like this:

Thank you very much for spending time with me in the interview. Even though I was somewhat nervous, I hope I was able to effectively respond to your questions. Our interview just reinforced my desire to work for ABC Co., and I look forward to hearing from you in the near future.

Sincerely,
Cathy Wilson

If you don't hear anything back from the interviewer in a couple of weeks, a short note to the interviewer reinforcing your interest in the organization and desire for obtaining the position would be quite appropriate. Sometimes the process drags on or is delayed. Your follow-up is a positive sign.

Best Practice

The first interview is difficult just because it is the first. You will get better.

Using the four steps—*preparation, practice, execution, and follow up*—will help you land that first job and others in the future.

Notes

_____

_____

_____

_____

_____

_____

_____

_____

_____

_____

_____

_____

SECTION THREE: FOCUS YOUR EFFORT

* Multitasking versus Focused Effort
Both approaches are effective, if used appropriately.

* Focus, Focus, Focus
Getting rid of all those distractions is the key to best results in a shorter time.

* Attention to Detail
What's on the surface may not tell you the whole story. Peel back that onion and dig!

* A Place for Everything and Everything in Its Place
How organization saves you time, speeds up your work, and reduces frustration.

* Look, Listen, Learn
You too can learn to be a sponge. Utilizing the three Ls in an active versus passive way will speed up your ability to become more and more productive.

* Close the Loop
It's not over til it's over. Getting the job completely done is what you are after. Being satisfied with 70–80 percent may result in failure.

* PPP: Prepare, Practice, Present
Here's a simple approach to make an effective presentation. All steps are important, especially the *practice* one.

* Ethics and Ethical Behavior
These are ten principles of ethical behavior. They will work in any work situation or environment. Doing the right thing is your guide.

* Building Relationships
Listed are some pointers to help you belong and participate.
Developing good relationships on and off the job will make work
more rewarding and playtime more fun.

* Be the Best
The fastest and most direct road to success is being the best you
can be at whatever you do. This will be recognized and rewarded.
No matter what the job, no matter what the career, by being the
best, you will achieve job satisfaction and advance.

Notes

_____

_____

_____

_____

_____

_____

_____

_____

_____

_____

_____

Treat your colleagues, family and friends with respect dignity, fairness and courtesy.

—Lorii Myers

The best teamwork comes from men who are working independently toward one goal in unison.

—James Cash Penney

Doing the best at this moment puts you in the best place for the next moment.

—Oprah Winfrey

The difference between who you are and who you want to be is the work you put in.

—Author Unknown

The only way to do great work is to love what you do. If you haven't found it yet, keep looking. Don't settle.

—Steve Jobs

MULTITASKING VERSUS FOCUSED EFFORT

Everybody multitasks. Why not? We can get things done faster and waste less time. Doesn't everyone say "time is money"? Why not fill every minute as best we can? I can easily do two or three things at a time. I can read, listen to music, check e-mail, text, and talk on the phone all at the same time.

Background

Most studies dispel the notion that multitasking automatically saves time or is really an effective way to get things done.
"It has been successfully demonstrated that the brain cannot effectively or efficiently switch between tasks, so you lose time. It takes four times longer to recognize new things, so you're not saving time. Multitasking actually costs time."[1]

Multitasking is not always the answer to getting things done faster, more efficiently, with the highest level of quality.
In today's world of ADD (attention deficit disorder), you might think that multitasking accommodates those who have a hard time focusing. Studies also show that too is incorrect.[2]

When to Multitask
For those who like to do many activities at once, multitask when...

1. the quality or outcome of the activity isn't critical;
2. the result of the activity doesn't affect others, especially customers;
3. the activity doesn't require a lot of thinking; and

---

[1] R. Rogers and Moresell, *Journal of Experimental Psychology: General* 124 (1995): pages 207–231.

[2] Joshua S. Rubenstein, "Executive Control of Cognitive Processes in Task Switching," (2001): pages 763-797.

4. the finished product, if needing a fix, isn't hard to fix.

When to Focus Your Effort
There is a time to really focus when...

1. the quality of the work performed is critical,
2. your outcome will affect a customer or others,
3. the activity does require thought and analysis, and
4. the outcome needs to be right the first time.

Best Practice

Multitasking can help get several things done concurrently, such as those not requiring serious thought, a lot of coordination, or a high level of quality.
Focused effort requires concentration and thought, which delivers a higher-quality product. Both approaches have effective applications. Their balanced use will benefit you in the long run.

Notes

_____

_____

_____

_____

FOCUS, FOCUS, FOCUS

As stated in a previous best practice, there is a time to multitask and a time to focus. Understanding when to use one approach or the other is important.

1. When quality is critical, focus.
2. When the outcome affects a customer or others, focus.
3. When the activity requires thought or analysis, focus.
4. If the outcome needs to be right the first time, focus.

Why is it often difficult to *really* focus your time or efforts? Your work environment may not lend itself to allow it. Sometimes your workload is so heavy you can't find the time to focus. Continual distractions make it difficult (e-mails, phones, texts, social media, meetings).
Setting priorities and meeting expectations is a balancing act that's tough to accomplish.
Can focusing on one project cause you to miss completing another?

All these and other reasons may be affecting your ability to focus. Those reasons can be mitigated, avoided, or even eliminated. When you feel that you have too many balls in the air, or, you can't do it all, or you are making too many mistakes with what you have, try these approaches to help focus your efforts and get stuff done.

Environment
Find a place where you can go to hide from distractions. This can be a place where you aren't known, a place that

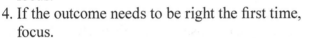

has a door, or just a place you won't be bothered or interrupted. Select a place that is comfortable. If others are around, let them know you need this time to focus and ask them to "please do not interrupt." Try to eliminate other potential interruptions. Turn off the world around you! Headphones can help.

Time
Allocate a block of time each day or week that is for focused work. That time is sacred, with no interruptions, and your time is dedicated to focus on the subject at hand. I have found sixty to ninety minutes is often the maximum for good, uninterrupted, focused work. Then stop. If more time is needed, take a break and return after coming up for air.

Organize
Gather all you need to use your focused time effectively. Take your lists, computer, documents, etc., etc.—all the tools and resources— that will be needed.
Select from your to do list what you want to complete first. Prioritize accordingly:

* Must do
* Want to do
* Like to do
* Someday will do
* Scratch it—won't do!

Zoom in and then drill down and work on that highest-priority item. Work on it until it is complete or you have accomplished what you want to complete in the allocated time. If this task is a large and complicated one, try to break it down into smaller pieces and bites and work on them. After one item is complete, move on to the next.

Best Practice

You can't focus on everything. That's not focus.

Selecting the most important task at hand and driving it to completion is not only an efficient use of time but also rewarding. You got it done, and it is a quality product.

These successful people have it right:

* "To create something exceptional, your mind set must be relentlessly focused on the smallest detail." (Giorgio Armani)

* "Stay focused, go after your dreams and keep moving toward your goal." (LL Cool J)

* "Concentrate all your thoughts upon the work at hand. The sun rays do not burn until brought to a focus." (Alexander Graham Bell)

* "Productivity is never an accident. It is always the result of a commitment to excellence, intelligent planning, and focused effort." (Paul J. Meyer)

Notes

_____

_____

_____

_____

_____

_____

_____

ATTENTION TO DETAIL

Deadlines are tough to meet!
Often, there is a natural tendency to have to settle for "run with what I have, that's as good as I can make it."
Do you find there is never enough time? Enough time to do it right?
Enough time to get into the details?

Background

Understanding the big picture is usually easier, more expedient, more fun, and less difficult to comprehend. Looking at the headline stories on the Internet or *USA Today* gives you an overview, a high-level interpretation of what the writer wants to communicate. It usually is a thirty-thousand-foot view that is designed to tell you something within a limited time frame or limited number of words.

However, in performing your work, getting *into the details* provides you with the necessary information that will help you make right decisions and do the best overall job. Doing it right is what you are paid to do! The more detail, the more focus, the higher probability you will effectively complete the task.

Don't let your big-picture thinking stop you from caring about the small stuff. Paying attention to the details could give you a competitive advantage. Details matter. It's worth getting it right.
—Steve Jobs, Apple Inc.

The larger the project, the more important the decision or task, the more *attention to detail* will help you ensure success.

When drilling down into the details, here are some things to think about:

1. Focus and *eliminate distractions* or other projects. Think only of this task or project. Focus, focus, focus!
2. Do big things in small chunks. Try to *break the task down* into small digestible pieces.
3. *Allow enough time* to drill down into the details. Your objective is to get it right. Speed is important; being thorough is more important.
4. *Peel back the onion* as you proceed. What you see on the surface may not be the reality or the truth.
5. *Document* and make lists of what you learn.
6. If you get tired of digging, *take a break* and walk away for a while. Come back and reread what you've learned and continue.
7. And last, *have another person take a look* at your work; a new set of eyes may see something and may find some errors.

There are many axioms, phrases, or quotations that emphasize the importance of paying attention to detail:

* "Watch the pennies and the dollars will take care of themselves." (Unknown Author)

* "The devil is in the details." (Unknown Author)

* "The devil is in the details, but so is salvation." (Hyman Rickover)

* "The *pursuit of excellence* [Lexus] comes with attention to details." (Toyota policy)

* "If you are going to achieve excellence in big things, you develop the habit in little matters." (Colin Powell)

* "When you work on the little things, big things happen." (Rodger Halston)

Best Practice

Attention to detail—by digging for and obtaining the detailed information to support your decisions, recommendations, or actions, you will greatly enhance the probability of doing it right. Remember, what is often on the surface may not be the whole story.

Notes

_____

_____

_____

_____

_____

_____

_____

_____

_____

_____

_____

A PLACE FOR EVERYTHING, AND
EVERYTHING IN ITS PLACE

Organizing and making visible important things will save you a lot of time, anxiety, and frustration. It is easy to do, it requires some effort and discipline, but it's worth it!

Background

We all have a lot of stuff. Some of it is needed every day, some not. Wasting a lot of time looking for the same things (over and over) is not very effective or efficient. Some examples:

1. Where are my keys, in my jacket, on my desk, in my chest of drawers?
2. I think I have enough cash in my wallet. Where is it?
3. My desk is a complete mess. I know the bill is there somewhere. Is it due? Past due?

4. I just can't find anything in my work area.
5. I am always running and can't find what I need.
6. And there are surely many more examples!

What is needed is a designated location so there is a place for everything and everything is in its place. After each use, the item is then returned to its place.
As I said before, this does require discipline.

Find a place to charge and keep that cell phone.
Ensure house and car keys are always returned to that same place.
Organize your desk so there is a place for each group of papers.
Post-its, notes, stickies—consolidate into one follow-up page; date it. Keep old pages as a record.

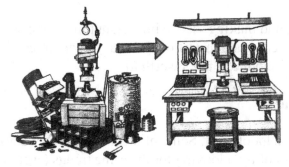

Look at that work area, can it be better organized? Take a look at your files and see how you can separate and organize them.
Where does that purse or wallet go when not in use?
A place for everything and everything in its place seems to be common sense, and it is. Doing it is another story. Failure to do it can have consequences.

"[Twenty-eight percent] of employers say they are less likely to promote someone with a disorganized workspace."[1]
"A coworker is judged based on the cleanliness of his or her workspace."[2]

Best Practice

Create a place for everything and put everything it its place. Save time, improve housekeeping, and reduce frustration.

---

[1] 2011 CareerBuilder Survey of 2662 hiring managers.

[2] 2012 Adecco survey, 1015 adults surveyed.

LOOK, LISTEN, LEARN

School is finished, so let's get on with it. No more studying, testing, practicing. Wrong!
You are just starting, maybe using some different methods, but you are just starting. Now you can have some fun without just reading, studying, and testing.

Background

Starting a new job can be interesting and difficult at the same time.
"What is really expected of me?"
"When I am stuck, who do I talk to?"
"If I ask too many questions, they'll think I am stupid or unprepared."
"Who really knows what's going on around here?"
"How am I going to be accepted by my coworkers?"
Sure, you'll have lots of questions and aren't expected to know everything as a new employee. No big deal.
But how you react to this *inexperience* will help determine how fast you get up to speed and what kind of performance you'll have.

Look
Watch those around you; pay close attention to the boss.
Look at your coworkers. They sure have more experience than you do.

 Look at how others do their job and how they interact among themselves, with the boss, and with customers.
Look for reactions of others to others, to yourself.
You have just joined a new group or team—look at what they do.

Listen

Hey, there is a lot of stuff going on around you. Listening to what is important is the key. Listen to what the boss says. Listen to your coworkers. And listen to your customers. Sorting through what is important and related to your job *is* the trick. This will come from experience, sometimes the experience of the first day.

Don't get trapped into listening to rumors, criticisms, negatives directed at the boss, coworkers, others.

With time and experience you will have time to form your own opinion about others. It is best to keep those opinions to yourself.

Learn

By looking and listening, you will learn. You will see what works and what may not. You'll learn that some people you work with are excellent (great performers, they enjoy their work, are hard workers, and are a *positive* influence in the workplace). Coworkers like to be around them, and you will too.

Others, you'll learn, are just the opposite. They can be very *negative*, criticize the workplace, the boss, the world, and usually aren't as productive as others. That is their choice. It surely should not be yours.

Best Practice

Walking into that new job looking, listening, and learning from others is an easy and effective way to quickly get up to speed, become part of the team, and determine what the best practices are, those best practices you might want to adopt.

Notes

_____

_____

_____

_____

CLOSE THE LOOP

"Boy, I was disappointed. I thought all was taken care of, and it wasn't. When I came in, it wasn't there. I thought you told me all was done and there was no problem. You said it'd be there."
"I am sorry. They told me it was all taken care of. When I left, they said all was set and it would be here for sure. I don't know what happened, but I'll find out."
What happened here? Or better yet, what didn't happen?

Background

When we join a work team, we become more and more reliant on others, and they on us! Getting a job done often requires a lot of coordination, timing, effective communication, and trust. When we make a promise or commitment, others will rely on it. Others will make plans or commitments on their own based on what we have said or promised.

Promises or commitments need to be locked in.
Promises or commitments should be *fail-safe*.[1]
Promises or commitments establish our credibility with coworkers and the boss or anyone receiving them.

Example
The young student had some timing difficulty obtaining the needed student loan that was due in two weeks.

Student: "My loan is approved, and it needs to be to the school by January 15. The money isn't available to them till February 1. The loan is approved but not available."

---

[1] "A system or plan that comes into operation in the event of something going wrong or that is there to prevent such an occurrence" (*The Oxford English Dictionary*).

Uncle: "Will the school accept a letter from the loan agent saying the loan is approved and that the school will wait till February 1 for the money? And if they agree, make sure you get the name and telephone number of the person you talked to who said it is okay."
Student: "I don't know, but I will call and get the information and the name."

Later in the day . . .

Student: "Yes, the school will accept the letter from the loan agent, and I'll be okay till February 1."
Uncle: "That's great. When will the letter be sent to the school?"
Student: "They promised to send it Wednesday, January 13 and will be at the school by January 20, and I'll be okay."
Uncle: "That's good. Who did you talk to, and what's his number?"

All seems set, there are no problems, the letter is to go out in three days and be at the school in plenty of time. The actual loan will be at the school before February 1—no problem. On January 12, the uncle calls the student.

Uncle: "Do you know if the letter will be sent out tomorrow, January 13?"
Student: "That's the plan. I assume they will do as they promised."
Uncle: "What is the name and telephone number of the person [Tim] you spoke to?"

Uncle calls Tim, the loan officer. After three attempts and no replies, he calls the general number of the bank.

Uncle: "Hello, I am calling about loan number xyz for my niece to see if Tim has sent the letter to the university, as promised. *Today* is the date for it to be sent."
Bank Officer (Jane): "I am sorry, I don't know anything about it. Tim has been off, ill for a week, and his work has been piling up. I am sorry, I know nothing about a letter."

Oooops!

After the uncle's lengthy explanation, Jane searched through Tim's desk, found the approved student loan application.

Jane: "Today is January 13, and I'll need to have someone draft the letter and send it to the university. That will take till January 18, and probably won't be to them by January 20
Uncle: "Please fax it to them, and I'll get you the fax number, okay?"
Jane: "Will do, but you do know that now because of the delay, we will not be able to get the money to the school by February 2! It just can't be done."
Uncle: "This defeats the whole purpose of all we have tried to do. The school must have the money by February 1, or my niece won't be able to enroll."
Jane: "I will have to see what I can do and will be back to you."
Uncle: "When?"
Jane: "Tomorrow."

That same afternoon . . .

Uncle (to the school admissions officer): "Our loan has been approved, and because of their loan officer's illness, they may not be able to have funds to you by February 1. What can we do?"
School Admin. Officer: "Once you talk with the bank officer tomorrow, let me know what she *can* do and give me her name and number, then I can see what I *can* do."

Next day . . .

Uncle: "Any news, any progress?"
Jane: "We can speed up the process, but the money will be delivered February 4 at best."
Uncle: "I will have the school admissions officer call you, okay? Maybe we can work something out."

That day, the bank officer and the school admissions officer spoke and agreed that 2/4 would work and the niece could enroll on February 1. The uncle asked for and obtained a faxed letter confirming this agreement, the niece enrolled on February 1, and the  admissions office received the funds on February 4 as promised!

Best Practice

Sometimes the best intentions run into unintended problems or poor performance by others. We can't let these variables affect our ability to get things done.

By anticipating what can or will go wrong, we learn to not assume all will work to plan. By identifying failure points and checking on them or eliminating them, we can reduce our risk. In the case of the student loan, after much expediting and follow-up, we were able to close the loop and guarantee the niece's admission. The final agreement document sealed the effort.

"It's not over til it's over," some wise person said.

Notes

_____

_____

_____

_____

_____

_____

PPP: PREPARE, PRACTICE, PRESENT

At some point you will be asked to make a pitch, presentation, or report to a group. Maybe it is a pitch to the boss, your coworkers, or a customer. Everyone gets a bit nervous when they have to stand up in front of a group (all alone!) and sound like they know what they are talking about.

These thoughts may run through your mind:

"What makes me the expert?"
"Do I really know what I am talking about?"
"What am I going to say?"
"What if I forget something?"
"What if someone asks me a question I can't answer?"
"How am I going to talk for five to ten minutes?"

Background

There are three phases to being effective in making a presentation:
One, prepare for the presentation.
Two, practice what you have prepared.
Three, present with support and confidence.

Prepare
Draft out a list of all the points you want to make in the presentation, the messages you want to deliver, in a few sentences or phrases.
Next, take this draft of points and decide what the best sequence for these points is so they are in the order in which you want to present them.
Look at the list again. Any points missed? Does this sequence seem to be the most effective for delivering your message?
(Don't hesitate to put some notes or reminders on your sheet related to your points.)

Practice

This is probably the most important step in preparing for a presentation. It is time to practice, practice, practice.

First, stand up alone and practice by yourself. Say a few introductory words about your topic and then start going through your presentation points.

Second, find a friend or associate (someone that is objective and somewhat knowledgeable about the topic) and ask them to listen to the pitch. Have them ask you questions about the presentation. Ask them to give you honest feedback as to what went well and, maybe, what did not go well. Ask them, "What three things am I doing well in the pitch, so I can keep doing them, and what three things can I do better or improve upon, so I can sharpen the presentation?" If there are no improvements recommended, push back until you get some suggestions (or find another friend or associate to help).

(Remember: Practice is the most important part of a presentation. You will feel more comfortable, more confident, and more relaxed as you do the final presentation. High school basketball teams practice four to five hours for every one hour of playtime. Band members practice six to eight hours for every hour performing.)

Present

So now it is show time. You have a solid presentation. You have practiced and know what you will present. The content of your presentation is clear to you, and your comfort level is high. You are the expert on your presentation.

* Follow your key points and sequence.
* Have your notes with you for reference.
* Anticipate questions with answers.
* If asked a question and you know the answer, fine—reply. If you don't, say, "I don't know, but I will find out and get back to you."
* Avoid words like *always*, *never*, and *all* since most things aren't absolute.
* Keep your presentation on track; you are in the lead and in control.

* Close the presentation with a thank-you (probably a thank-you because it's over).

Best Practice

The experience of delivering a report or presentation does not have to be a bad one. Since it is *you that has been asked* to present, it is an *opportunity for you*, a positive opportunity. By diligently *preparing*, repeatedly *practicing*, and with confidence *presenting*, you will give an effective presentation, and don't be surprised if you will be asked to do one again!

Notes

_____

_____

_____

_____

_____

_____

ETHICS AND ETHICAL BEHAVIOR

In your workplace you will learn there are some behaviors that are acceptable and some unacceptable. Then again, there are behaviors promoted to help the organization meet its goals and objectives. You may even receive a list that spells them out for you—the dos and don'ts.

Background

There are some ethical principles that will guide you as you initiate your work experience. I call them the top ten for workplace success that, if followed, will provide you guidance no matter where you work and no matter what job you perform.

1. Honesty
2. Trust
3. Respect
4. Truth
5. Honor
6. Integrity
7. Understanding
8. Tolerance
9. Fairness
10. Kindness

As you read through the *definitions* and a boss's view, you'll quickly see that many of these are connected or interconnected. That's good, because they are.

Honesty
"Sincere, genuine, upright, and fair; honorable in principles, intentions, and actions."

I want my people to be honest. We rely on one another. If they aren't honest, how will we be able to work, solve problems, and get stuff done? Honesty is the best policy—should be the only one!

Trust
"Firm reliance, confidence, and belief; faith; custody and care of."
I trust you to take care of that. I trust you will make the right decision. What I am saying is, you take care of it—it's taken off my agenda. I'm not going to worry about it; you will.

Respect
"Deferential or high regard; to have esteem for—to pay one's respects."
Whoever you deal with—customers, suppliers, coworkers—listen, be fair, use good manners; treat others as you want to be treated. As Roger Federer (Swiss tennis champion) stated, "I fear no one, but I respect everyone."

Truth
"Conformity to knowledge, fact, or actuality; veracity; the real state of affairs."
When we know the truth, we can solve problems. We all make mistakes; don't cover them up. Make them visible, and we'll fix them. Tell the truth, or someone will tell it for you.

Honor
"Personal integrity maintained without legal or other obligation."
When it's decision time, do the right thing, honor the truth. It hurts everyone less in the long run.

Integrity
"Strict personal honesty and independence."
If you know the truth, stand by it. Stick to it; don't waver. Again, do what is right, no matter the pressure. How others see you is on the line! There is respect involved here.

Understanding
"A reconciliation of differences; an agreement reached between two or more persons or groups; tolerant or sympathetic."
Understanding your coworkers' point of view is important. It's good to listen to and understand their perspective. You won't always agree, but you should appreciate how they look at things. We can agree to disagree, and that's okay too.

Tolerance
"The capacity for or practice of recognizing and respecting the opinions, practices, or behavior of others."
You will meet a lot of interesting people along the way—a lot of different, interesting people. Showing respect and understanding of others will go a long way. Put yourself in the other guy's shoes and see how they feel!

Fairness
"The quality or state of being fair; impartial treatment; just or equitable; consistent with rules."
Sure, life's not always fair, so we have policies, processes, and procedures (PPP) to help us run the operation. Follow them and you'll be okay. The three Ps help provide everyone a level playing field and the same chance. Play by the rules!

Kindness
"An act or instance of being kind; governed by consideration and compassion: friendly, obliging."
A simple smile, friendly hello, followed by a helping hand, sure goes a long way. Being tough, aggressive, and driven doesn't mean you can't be kind to others.
"It is nice to be important, but it is more important to be nice" (Alan Mulally, president of Ford Motor Co.).

Best Practice

The top ten for workplace success, as it relates to ethics and ethical behavior, are best practices in their own right. They provide a solid foundation as you build your work career. They will *not* always be

easy or convenient to follow, and others may not be so inclined to adhere to these principles. It's not a perfect world.
However, by their use, *you are doing the right thing*!

Notes

BUILDING RELATIONSHIPS

You probably won't believe this, but when you start working every day, you'll find you spend more time with fellow workers than with your friends or even your family. You can expect to spend eight to ten hours per day, sometimes six days a week, on the job.
It is important that you focus on developing good working relationships. If effectively done, those relationships will:

1. allow you to be happier and more productive;
2. make work more enjoyable—yes, even fun;
3. help you develop your career;
4. allow you to create good relationships with customers, suppliers, and other stakeholders;
5. position you for pay raises and promotions; and
6. help you attain your goals and provide real job satisfaction.

Remember, work is eight to ten hours per day, every day. Job satisfaction is very important.

Background

"You can submarine your career and work relationships by actions you take and the behaviors you exhibit at work. No matter your education, your experience, or your title, if you can't play well with others, you will never accomplish your work mission."[1]
Think of this, as a new member of the workforce, and maybe even a team, you will have a role to play. That role will be dependent on others as others will be depending on you. The maximum

[1]   Susan M. Heathfield, *Human Resources Management*. Acknowledged human resource expert.

or ultimate level of accomplishment will come about through effectively working together.

These are some cornerstones of building good working relationships:

* Trust
* Mutual respect
* Open, honest communications
* Listening
* Truthfulness

With these in mind, and with the appropriate application, here are fifteen practices that will help you develop those good working relationships:

1. Talk with your coworkers, not always just about work.
2. Smile and others will smile back.
3. Call people by their name; we all like it when we are recognized.
4. Be friendly and helpful.
5. Be cordial and positive. No one likes a whiner or a habitual complainer!
6. Be interested in your coworker. What is going on in their life, family, and friends?

7. Be generous with praise and stingy with criticism. Celebrate successes.
8. Listen to others. Listen twice as much as you speak.

9. Be thoughtful of others' opinions. Opinions are opinions.
10. Develop a sense of humor—laugh at yourself. Laughter shows you are human and maybe a bit humble.
11. Accept that you will make errors and mistakes. That's okay. Don't hide or cover up mistakes. Learn from them and move on.
12. Acknowledge others with a "Good morning," "How's it going," "What's up," "See you tomorrow," and "Thank you!"
13. Consider others' feelings when you speak and act; put yourself in your coworkers' shoes.
14. Avoid gossip, and only speak positively of others; if you can't, it is best to be quiet.
15. Don't try to find time, *but make time*, to get to know your coworkers. You *make the effort*. Visit their work area and see what they are doing.

Best Practice

Your work results and career are really dependent on being able to effectively work with others. Making the effort to grow and develop good working relationships will make you, your coworkers and team more successful.

BE THE BEST

"I want to be the best. I want to make a lot of money, like you. What is the secret? What should I study, major in? I want to be on my own. I want to be creative. I'd like to own my own business so I don't have a boss. I want to be my own boss and come and go as I please. I want time to do the things *I want to do*. How do I get there?"

Background

There are a lot of desires and questions here and a lot of wants. As a graduate, you probably have these questions and more running through your mind. Graduation day comes with a *big door* opening to you. How smoothly and effectively you pass through that door and where you go will change over time. Your path (education, jobs, careers, family) will evolve and change as you go.
Success story examples:

* I have a friend (a good student) who went to night school and community college and, after many years, finally graduated. He landed a job with a waste management company as a dispatcher. Through the years he was promoted to foreman, then manager, district manager, to vice president. *Being the best!*

* Another friend of mine survived college, served in the military (flew navy jets), went to work for the government, and moved up pay grades through his roles in the government. Years later, he joined a consulting company as vice president. Then he joined a think tank (as senior vice president) that services the government.

Many jobs, many great successes! *Being the best!*

* A relative of mine didn't graduate. After ninth grade, he had to go to work to support his family. He did this job, did that job. He went to work in a brewery—he drove a lift truck. He became a foreman. He moved to another business, learned the business, and years later he bought out the retiring owner. It took many years but he became his own boss, with his own company, with his own responsibilities. His career went from a ninth-grade graduate to president of his own small company. *Being the best!*

* I worked with a lady who, after high school, went to work wherever she could find a job. After some time, she was able to join the largest employer in the community as a clerk. She soon was promoted to a position requiring more responsibility as an administrative assistant. This person became the administrative assistant and coordinator for an executive vice president. She was at the top of her field and was recognized for it! *Being the best!*

* Edward was just an average student in high school. However, he was an excellent football player, always a starter, always the best. He became a teacher and coach. Eventually he became a college coach and won numerous championships. After retiring from working and coaching, he was recognized for outstanding coaching performance in the university's hall of fame. Three years later, he was recognized for outstanding performance (inducted into the hall of fame) as a player from the university from which he graduated. As a player and coach, he was *being the best!*

There are thousands, if not millions, of success stories like these. This is America!
What made these and others so successful? Is there a common thread? Common attributes? Education? Luck? Motivation? Job Satisfaction? Patronage? Money? Persistence? Perseverance?
How did they find their way, their right path, their path to success?

Best Practice

These people were hard workers at being the best in their job or their field. They differentiated themselves from others. Their work ethic, plus some of the attributes listed, helped them become very successful.
Being the best at whatever you do, no matter what you do, will lead to recognition, reward and success.

Notes

_____

_____

_____

_____

_____

_____

SECTION FOUR: MOVING FORWARD, STEPPING UP

* Meetings! Meetings! Meetings!
Whether you are running the meeting or just attending, make sure there is value in the time spent off the job. Getting something out of the meeting is up to you. It is *your time* off the job.

* Up Close and Personal
Being in the best position to listen, learn, participate, and be recognized. No back row for you!

* Volunteer: Be a Leader
Don't hesitate to volunteer if you feel you can contribute and make a difference. If asked to lead, why not?

* The Black Hole
You don't want to go there. Once you do, your reputation will be hard to repair, and those depending on you will hesitate to trust you.

* Step-by-Step
How do you handle a big project that is complicated and complex? How do you get it done in the designated time frame? Let me introduce the elephant.

* Practicing CPI
Never give up. You may be slowed down. There may be obstructions before you. Others may fail you. The target may change or be delayed. But you never give up till it is done.

* Measure It
Five steps to help you reach that goal, that target. Keeping score and keeping results visual works in sports, education, health, etc., etc. In your work environment, measures are critical.

* The Five Whys
Here is a basic process created and used by Toyota in all their operations. The process works and is easy to use in searching for the root cause.

* Give Me More
Shock the boss and ask for more work when you are ready for it. Why not use that free time and get something done?

None of us is as smart as all of us.
—Ken Blanchard

When you get into a tight place and everything goes against you, never give up then, for that is just the place and time that the tide will turn.
—Harriet Beecher Stowe

Tell me and I forget. Show me and I remember. Involve me and I understand.
—Chinese Proverb

If you are only doing what you are getting paid for, and doing it no better than the average employee, then your pay is most likely right where it should be.
—Bo Bennett

MEETINGS! MEETINGS! MEETINGS!

"Why should I, we, spend so much time in meetings? They take so long and are a waste of time. I have my job to do and meetings put me behind, and it will be hard to catch up. So what's the big deal with so many meetings (team meetings, staff meetings, planning meetings, communication meetings, etc., etc.)? Should I go, or skip them?"

Go!

Background

Meetings do take time and energy, and they take you away from your immediate job, your responsibility. However, meetings prove very valuable if handled correctly and efficiently. Here's why. Most bosses, leaders, or coworkers call for meetings to...

1. gather or impart information to a group (this is done more efficiently and with less chance of error if done one by one);
2. exchange ideas, views, opinions and suggestions (open discussion also generates ideas that may not be created by one person alone—diversity of inputs is powerful);

Creating a Plan

3. discuss options, narrow those options, and obtain support and buy-in;
4. collectively solve problems;
5. make decisions and move forward;
6. create a plan to do what is necessary (in an organized way) to make decisions; or
7. communicate, communicate, communicate (this is talking, listening, and discussing; meetings are chances to give *your*

input and help provide direction that affects the organization and *you*).

In these meetings you can learn a lot more than by just using e-mails, texts, or other non-face-to-face methods.

In face-to-face meetings, you will:

1. see the body language of others (this form of communication provides insight sometimes as valuable as verbal communication).
2. be engaged (just by being in the meeting, you will be expected to participate and contribute).
3. be able to ask questions, hear the questions of others, and hear the answers.
4. get all to participate, if the meeting is handled properly (also, buy-in is often easier to obtain in meetings and usually more timely; a sense of belonging grows, and usually, a form of bonding is developed).
5. often have opportunities at visualization (charts, graphs, handouts, use of whiteboards, etc., etc.) that will help with understanding and explanations.
6. sometimes find the time spent is less—collectively spent—than alone for both you and the person running the meeting.

From many perspectives, meetings are value added if properly organized and managed. If senior management felt they were a waste of time and they were making you less productive or efficient, they would not support or drive them. Go and participate in meetings.

Here are some suggestions for meeting effectiveness—whether you are calling the meeting or you are helping with a meeting implementation. These are simple but effective:

1. Create an agenda with timelines. Keep the meeting as short as possible. Short is better (fifteen minutes, thirty minutes, one hour, two hours—beyond this, it gets risky).
2. Invite participants, not spectators. Keep the size of the group small.

3. Start on time. If this is to be a regular (weekly, monthly, etc.) meeting and participants are often late, install a fine system. At 1:00 p.m., the meeting starts, the door is closed. Late arrivals pay a dollar for late arrival. This dollar could be put into some celebration fund for future use. Lateness will cease to be a problem.

4. Have someone be the note taker, someone who isn't running the meeting.

5. Focus on the topics on the agenda. Stop any straying discussions. Turn off phones!

6. Try to engage all in the discussions. Call on those who say nothing or aren't engaged.

7. Capture and summarize what is decided on each topic so everyone understands and there is no later disagreement.

8. Where action is required after the meeting, seek out volunteers to carry forward the work needing to be done before the next meeting.

9. Create a draft agenda for the next meeting and send to all after the meeting.

10. After the meeting has ended, spend some time to evaluate the meeting as to effectiveness (after-action review):

   a. What were the objectives of the meeting? Were those objectives met?

   b. What went well in the meeting? Make sure you continue those practices or approaches.

   c. What could be improved on in the meeting? What should we do differently?

   d. What will we do in the next meeting to make it more effective?

Best Practice

There is a place for e-mails, texting, and teleconferencing. These tools are usually fairly effective at passing along information. However, they are rather restrictive at capitalizing on interactive inputs, collective use of intellects, and the problem-solving capabilities of the group. *Attend and participate in meetings.* And when you lead a meeting, follow the guidelines listed. Successful meetings generate successful solutions and generate better results!

Notes

_____

_____

_____

_____

_____

_____

_____

UP CLOSE AND PERSONAL

Here we go, back to those meetings. Do you ever wonder who is doing all the work around here? All we seem to do is go to meetings.

Most meetings are really focused on communication of one sort or another. The boss (or someone) feels it is important to pull the workers together and pass on some information or instructions. So someone thinks it *is important* to take you off the job and communicate.

Background

Since you are now off the job and *have to* sit through another one of these meetings, should you take advantage of the free time and slip to the back of the office or room and sit with *your* buddies as a way to get through this? Catch up on e-mail?

No!

Sit up front, preferably in the front row. Get to a position close to the speaker so you can clearly hear and see everything.

Here are some of the advantages of being up close and personal:

1. You will plainly hear what the speaker is saying.
2. You will have less or no distractions between you and the speaker.

3. You will focus on the speaker and be able to see his expressions and emphasis points.
4. You will better see charts, graphs, or other visual tools used.
5. You will be able to take better notes.
6. Questions are more easily handled coming from the front row.
7. And the speaker will see you and see *you are engaged*!

Here are some disadvantages of being up close and personal:

1. It will be hard to not follow the speaker.
2. Your mind won't so easily wander.
3. If you doze off, you'll be seen or noticed.
4. Your friends will miss you back in the last row.
5. The speaker will see you way back there and wonder *if you are engaged* or not.

Obviously, the advantages of being a front-row participant greatly outweigh all disadvantages. And besides, you may learn something, something important.

Best Practice

In meetings, lectures, and presentations, be a front-row participant. You will hear more, see more, learn more, and be better informed. *Up close and personal* works!

VOLUNTEER: BE A LEADER

I always liked the situation created when the commander said, as ten soldiers lined up before him, "I need a volunteer to lead a small team. It is an important mission, and I need someone to lead. So those of you who'll volunteer, please take one step forward."
All took one step *back*, except one person, who was caught off guard. The commander said, "Well, I guess I have my volunteer!"

Background

There will be opportunities to lead, and some will step forward, others hold back. Of course there is anxiety related to leading. *Where do I start? Will I know what to do? Will I be able to get the job done? Will the team listen to me? What happens if we fail? Do I have the skills to lead? Why should I volunteer? Let someone else do it!*
You are asking the right questions, questions that will get answered as you lead an effort or team.
Leading can be viewed as an inborn skill set or one that comes about through a process of teaching, learning, observing, and practicing. Many experts believe that leadership is one-third born and two-thirds made. And those in the one-third born supposedly inherited attributes such as being extroverted, highly organized, effective at communications, and/or other special traits. Note, these traits also can be learned, practiced, and fine-tuned.
Volunteering to lead an effort will give you an opportunity to take initiative, work with others, develop your organizational and people skills, and take on an assignment that the boss sees as important. This is an opportunity, not a burden!

Getting Started: Getting Organized
Before calling the team together, make sure some of the basics are in place with the boss as to what exactly the assignment is:

1. What is the project description and scope?
2. What is the timeline? When is the job to be done?
3. What is the expected finished product?
4. Who is the customer of the product?
5. Who is on the team?
6. Other.

Once these are clarified with the boss, follow these steps as you work through the leadership project.

Premeeting
The assignment will take time and effort. Make time for it. Allocate the necessary time for planning, meetings, communications, etc. The key word is *make*.
Establish a place for meetings—away from other distractions.
Get to know your team, their background, skills, interests, time availability.

First Meeting
* Schedule that first meeting to get organized and communicate the assignment information from the boss. Clarify, listen, discuss, again listen, and seek input from all on the team about going forward. That first meeting should be casual, open, and a time to share information. Have a crisp short agenda—not too long.
* At that first meeting, some assignments should be made to gather information or to plan the next steps. At minimum, you need to establish when and where the next meeting will be (I like to make a shift from calling them meetings to *huddles*!)
* Between huddles, continue to communicate progress, learnings, issues, and other factors associated with the assignment. Keeping the assignment center stage is important.

Subsequent Meetings, or Huddles

* Repeatedly emphasize and reinforce that you want all to participate. Ask all for ideas and input.
* Being open and honest is necessary for all. Everyone will participate, and the work will be shared. Delegate and don't try to do all the work yourself.
* Working as a team is what's required since the team solution will be better than just an individual's; if the boss didn't think this, he'd just give the assignment to one person.
* The team members who get their assignments done, recognize them with "Great, thank you." Those who don't get them done, ask questions as to why, when they will get the assignment done, and if they need help. Some assignments will be more difficult than others, but all are important to the success of the team.
* Keep the focus on the assignment. When someone gets off track, pull them back in or ask them to *park that topic* till the end of the huddle—when time will be available.
* Discuss and make decisions and move forward.
* Keep records of huddles and assignments. Assign someone the job.
* Periodic reviews and updates with the boss prove helpful and can ensure alignment.
* It is absolutely a good idea to have some fun as you work in the huddle. *High fives* can go a long way to signify progress or success.
* With every huddle, make assignments and set the next huddle time and date.
* It is always a good practice to end the huddle with a quick reminder as to what the assignment is and the target date for completion.

Completing the Assignment
As the leader, you should be the first to recognize the completion of the assignment. Go back to what the boss gave as basics and confirm with the team if *all objectives were met*. If so, then schedule a huddle with the team and the boss for review and celebration of the completed project. Each team member should

participate in reviewing the work done and credit should be shared by all. The team leader often takes a backstage role and allows each team member to be recognized by the boss.

Say something to say to each team member, *congratulations and thank you.* *This* will be appreciated by all.

Best Practice

Volunteering and volunteering to lead is an opportunity to learn about the organization, about or from the boss, from others, and about yourself. Leadership skills come from getting over the anxiety of the unknown and from practicing what you've observed and learned.
Taking that step forward becomes easier, and your volunteering effort *is recognized* by the boss.

Notes

_____

_____

_____

_____

_____

THE BLACK HOLE

We all know what it is. Sometimes stuff seems to go to that *imaginary place in which things are lost*, that ever-lurking, dangerous black hole!

Background

The boss asks you to do something, take care of something, or make sure something happens. That something is important to the boss. He has entrusted you to get it done.

The boss thinks you are working on it, expects it will be done, and is waiting for its completion. Finally he remembers he asked you to take care of this weeks ago and now confronts you with, "Whatever happened to that project I asked you for? I need it for tomorrow so I can finish my report!" Ooops, the project fell into that black hole.

Your coworker gives you her report that you need to prepare for your joint project. You know she gave you her section, but where is it? It will be embarrassing to ask her for another copy. You seem to ask her often to redo her work, to help you.

You are right, your coworker is already saying, "Here we go again, it's lost in that black hole. His black hole is going to affect my performance too if our project is late!"

The black hole is not really a place. In fact, it is the opposite of a place; it is an unknown. It is a mysterious void. You really don't want to visit the black hole—whatever it is.

Some simple rules that help you not to visit there:

1. When someone asks you to do something, *write it down* and follow up on it. If you have a target date, or not, and if that request is not fulfilled, let the requestor know the status.
2. Get *organized* and have a place for everything and everything in its place. Keep the assignment visible and in front of you.
3. Assignments should have target *completion dates*; mark your calendar with the assignment and the date to be done.
4. Plan and work to get all assignments done *early*. I have never been criticized for getting something done a day or so early.
5. And lastly, *never* say "It must have gone into that black hole." It's just an excuse. Not knowing where something is looks bad and is bad. Your credibility will be affected and others' confidence in you will diminish.

Best Practice

When you get an assignment, write it down, keep record of its progress, work to a target date, get it done early, and keep the customer of the assignment up-to-date as to the status. *Don't use or visit that black hole!*

STEP-BY-STEP

How many times have you been asked to do something that seems overwhelming, complicated, and unrealistic? The job is so big and you don't have a clue where to start. You may ask yourself, "How am I ever going to get that done in the time I've got? There is just no way."

Background

"I want you to inventory everything in the entire warehouse. I want nothing missed. I need to know what's in there, no mistakes, and I don't care how long it takes. Just get it right."
This is what the boss wants and expects. Where do you start, and what needs to be done? This is a *big* project and, to the boss, a *big* deal!

Do remember, "You can't eat the elephant all at once." You need to establish a good plan, one that is realistic and doable, and carry that plan forward, step-by-step. See the section on *what's your plan.*

The boss has set your goal: complete, accurate inventory.
You can establish your strategy.
You can establish your plan.
You can determine the tactics.
You can set a target date for completion.
You can measure your results and progress.

Possible step-by-step plan:

1. Step 1 (overall strategy): *I don't want to take the inventory on the weekend but could take some each evening. Maybe two to three hours per day after work. I can get two others to help with the counting, the scales and inventory tags.*
2. Step 2 (basic plan): *Our small team will go and determine (estimate) how long this project will take. We'll estimate all the equipment, tools, tags, etc., etc., based on what we see as the project's scope.*
3. Step 3 (tactics): *We will order all the stuff needed for the inventory. Once we have it all, we'll schedule the inventory. We estimate it will take five days to do, and we'll divide the warehouse into five equal sections. Everyone will be notified to save that two to three hours per day.*
4. Step 4 (measures and target date): *Starting on Monday next week, we should have it done by late Friday. One-fifth of the inventory should be done each day. If by some chance our estimates are off or we run into problems, we can spill into Saturday or the next Monday.*

This is a good step-by-step plan. You have taken what seemed to be a huge project and have broken it down into small, manageable steps. The overall plan is shown to the boss; he approves it and is impressed with your thoughtfulness and coordination.

Best Practice

Creating a good plan with a *step-by-step process* grabs that elephant and brings him down to size!

PRACTICING CPI

Most of us know what CPR stands for and how it helps in an emergency. Practicing CPI is quite different. It just means "never giving up"!

Background

There will be times when you'll face so many obstacles to meeting your assignment, goal, or target that you'll feel it is unattainable and you might as well give up. "I've wasted so much time already trying to get it done, no use in wasting more time." You may say, "I've hit that brick wall and that's it!" "Maybe I'll turn it over to the boss!?"
CPI can help.
The *C* stands for being *consistent* ("marked by an unchanging position"). As you try and try to get something done, if you are consistent with your effort and drive, the goal will become clearer and one that is within sight. Your position will become visible to others.
The *P* stands for being *persistent* ("continuing in a course of action without regard to opposition or previous failure"). Aggressive follow-up often refers to persistence. Some may call this stubbornness. Others may call it focused on purpose and results.
The *I* stands for being *insistent* ("standing or resting on something; not budging"). Here we are taking a firm position, one based on facts and one from which we will not waver.

Example of CPI Use

Our supplier has periodically failed to ship our supplies to us on time. Some weeks he is two or three days early. Others he is a week late, sometimes jeopardizing our production line and maybe affecting customer delivery. We can't continue like this. My job is to have what is needed every Monday. My performance depends on Monday deliveries.

C—Each week I give the supplier my scheduled needs. On Tuesday I will provide the schedule of materials needed. I will have the schedule to my supplier by 10:00 a.m. every Tuesday. *Every Tuesday at 10:00 a.m.*

P—On Tuesday, I will call my supplier at ten thirty and confirm that he has received the schedule, that all is understood on the schedule, and that he confirms there is no problem meeting the schedule for next Monday's noon delivery. Issues are discussed and resolved, ending with the supplier's commitment for Monday's delivery. If there are any unresolved issues or concerns revealed by the supplier, I'll ask, "Who do I talk to that can guarantee me my deliveries?" If required, I will then talk to the more responsible person who confirms delivery. If that confirmation isn't established at this level, I will continue *climbing the ladder* until I will get the commitment.

I—On Friday, I will call my supplier and confirm the shipment is on schedule and okay for Monday. If all is okay, I will plan another call for Monday to confirm the shipment is in transit and will be delivered. If for some reason the shipment will be late or maybe missed till Tuesday, I will call the person who made the commitment and find out where the problem is and when it will be fixed. If not satisfied with the answer, I may continue to *climb the ladder* to the president's office, if needed.

Remember, my performance is pegged to the supplier's performance. I must get the material needed; others are depending on me. By being consistent, persistent, and insistent, I am letting the supplier know I am after the material and I will not give up till I have it.

Best Practice

Having a balanced approach that shows you are consistent (reliable and regular), you are persistent (won't take the eye off the ball), and insistent (just won't give up) instills a high degree of confidence in your performance and ability to ensure the job will get done. CPI gets results!

If you have an important point to make, don't try to be subtle or clever. Use a pile driver. Hit the point once. Then come back and hit it again. Then hit it a third time—a tremendous whack.
—Winston Churchill

Notes

_____

_____

_____

_____

_____

_____

MEASURE IT

It seems like anything very important is supported by measurement. We measure sports (scores, individual performance averages, win-loss records), education (grades, SAT scores, GPAs), diets (calories, fats, carbohydrates, weight), medical labs (cholesterol, blood pressure, etc., etc.), and work (attendance, project deadlines, performance).

We are surrounded by measurements that provide us a track record.

Background

It is hard to imagine putting a lot of effort toward anything and not measuring *how you are doing.* This applies to not only our work environment, but also with our personal goals and objectives. There is a lot of truth to "If you measure it, you'll get it; if you don't, you won't." That sounds pretty absolute, and of course, it is not. However, when we measure, we do the following:

1. *Focus*—attention is paid to the most important.
2. *Improve vision*—trends, problems, and variation jump out and opportunities are identified.
3. *Make good or better decisions*—seeing in black-and-white provides us with the facts and data needed to make good decisions, decisions that are not just opinion based.

One of the best approaches to create measures to help you is
* first, defining your goal or target (what is it that you want to accomplish or attain?);
* second, creating a metric (for each goal or target, define how you can measure your progress and be able to see if you are moving in the right direction);
* third, establishing a system (keep a scorecard, a tracking system, where you can measure where you are against your goal);

* fourth, posting the results (do this daily, weekly, whatever makes sense, so you can see the trend; keep this visible—right in front of you—so it isn't missed); and
* fifth, reviewing the results and adjusting (if your progress is satisfactory, keep on; if not, make a change that might get you back on track or speed up the progress).

Simple Real-Life Example
John, a coworker, wanted to lose weight and get to 200 pounds. For him this was an admirable and aggressive target (he was at 247 pounds.).
He used these five steps:

1. Goal: 200 pounds
2. Metric: pounds
3. System: weighing himself first thing in the morning every morning
4. Posting of results: a little chart near the scale where numbers are written
5. Review of results and adjustments: from 247 to 245, 240, 239, 241, 238, etc., etc. He got down to 220, then John went on vacation (ooops). John shot up to 225.

There was an adjustment needed (no pizza and beer). Back on track, John went to 224, 220, 210, etc., etc.
Eventually his plan worked as he reached the 200-pound goal. He continued the system, and now his weight stays around 200, with periodic *adjustments*!
You will sooner or later hear the term *KPI* (key performance indicators). This is a phrase to emphasize the use of measures and not have too many. The goal is to measure the few and only the important.

Best Practice

Measuring and keeping score are important tools that will help you know where you are, where you are going, and determine if you are making the progress you want. Many organizations have realized that using continuous improvement systems like JIT, Lean, and Six Sigma rely heavily on measures and measurement, and their use is key to an organization's success.

Notes

_____

_____

_____

_____

_____

_____

_____

THE FIVE WHYS

Toyota Motor Company is regularly recognized as the "best, highest quality" automobile manufacturer in the world.[2] In the last five years, Toyota produced more automobiles than any other manufacturer.[3] The Lexus (*pursuit of perfection*) each year wins awards as the best-built, highest-quality car.

When you analyze the reasons for this tremendous and consistent success, you will quickly realize that a key ingredient is the Toyota Production System (TPS).

There are many documented elements to TPS—build quality in, just-in-time, kanban, elimination of waste, and many, many more that created a fully integrated system. I want to tell you about one of those elements.

Background

Training of Toyota team members and teams goes on consistently within the Toyota plants. The individual and the team play important roles in building the automobiles, and this is recognized and enforced in each plant operation. Problems are a continual fact of day-to-day life in an assembly plant. Therefore, each team member is trained and provided tools to help solve problems. One basic tool is *asking the five whys.*

The five whys is a process of arriving at the real problem cause through investigation of all possible causes. Here we filter through the superficial causes and arrive at the root cause. Once that root cause is identified, the appropriate fix can be established and installed.

---

2   *Forbes Magazine*'s Top 10 Quality Cars 2011 (five out of the ten).

3   *The Telegraph*, March 19, 2014 (Number 1 in the world 2008–2013).

Remember, with TPS, team members are after the ultimate source of the problem. The way to do this is to keep asking why (get a response), another why (get a response)—starting with the problem—and keep asking the *why*, going from the possible cause to the real cause.

A couple of examples
Late Deliveries
Problem statement: *We continue to miss customer deliver dates, and the customer is upset!*
Why 1: *Why do we keep missing the schedule delivery dates? (Because parts aren't produced and ready to ship on time.)*
Why 2: *Why aren't the parts produced and ready to ship on time? (Because production says they don't have the material to produce the parts early enough.)*
Why 3: *Why doesn't production have the parts on time to produce the parts? (Because the supplier ships the parts too late.)*
Why 4: *Why does the supplier ship parts too late? (Because the supplier doesn't know what we need until it's too late.)*
Why 5: *Why doesn't the supplier know our needs and their timing? (Because we stopped giving the supplier forecasts with lead times.)*
Why 6: *Why did we stop forecasting needs to suppliers? (Because Mary retired and we stopped forecasting needs when she did.)*

These *six* whys uncovered the root cause of the problem. We were not giving the supplier forecasts of our needs and adequate lead times to meet those needs.

Stranded
Problem statement: *You are on the way home from work and your car stops in the middle of the highway.*
Why 1: *Why did your car stop? (Because I ran out of gas.)*
Why 2: *Why did you run out of gas? (Because I didn't buy any gas on the way to work.)*
Why 3: *Why didn't you buy gas on the way to work? (Because I didn't have any money.)*

Why 4: *Why didn't you have money? (Because I lost all my money last night in a poker game.)*

Why 5: *Why did you lose all your money in last night's poker game? (Because I am not very good at bluffing when I don't have a good hand.)*

Root cause for this particular problem: a poor bluffer! The fix: learn to be a good bluffer or give up poker! (Maybe what was initially seen as a technical problem, in reality, is a human problem.)

There are some obvious benefits to using the five whys:

1. It is a simple, easy-to-use process.
2. It is an effective way to separate symptoms from causes, which will lead to the root cause.
3. The process provides you a comprehensive way to determine and expose the relationships between various problem causes.

4. You can use this process with a group or by yourself.
5. The process isn't expensive—you need your team, a flip chart, and time!

Best Practice

We all encounter problems in the workplace. Some of these problems appear to be simple and easy to correct. Those that are, we fix and get on with it.

However, those reoccurring problems may be the result of not finding the real or root cause. The five whys (or six, or seven, etc.) will allow you to uncover the cause and apply a fix that sticks!

GIVE ME MORE

"Do I really need eight hours to get the job done? The last lady that did this job took eight. If I start getting it done too early, they'll think the job is too easy and give me more work. If I get it done too quickly, others will say, 'Slow down, you are ruining it for the rest of us. We won't get our overtime.'"

Background

I can remember a coworker coming up to me and saying, "You are the new kid. You are working too hard, you better slow down. Leave some work for the second shift." At the same location on another day: "That work is not your job, that is another job classification. You need to stop what you are doing." Since I was the *new kid*, I did listen to the fellow workers, followed their advice, because I wanted to fit in.

Another job, while scheduling a department, I was able to *continuously improve* my work routine, and after some months, I completed my job in just six hours. Now I have two hours available to do what? Should I stretch the work out for eight hours or what? Should I tell someone? I told my boss; he smiled and gave me additional work and responsibility.

John was to go on vacation, and Phil was designated to fill in for two weeks. After some training, John left, and the job requirement was to make 150 pallets each night. Night one, Phil produced 145, the next 160, then 190, 220, 240. With a little sweat, Phil made 250 a night. Phil continued to make 250 a night while it got easier to do so.

The foreman, Ziggy (nice name), regularly saw the results of Phil's work and said to John on his return, "Why can't you get me 250 pallets per night?"

After some discussions, Phil and John got together, and John was able to easily increase his output to 200 pallets. The company and the boss benefitted.

Lastly, I remember a GM vice president (talking to a small group of young employees at the factory) tell us some stories about how he developed his career at GM. He said, "I wasn't the smartest, nicest, most polished guy, but I was always there to volunteer, to say 'I can do that. I'll do that too.' No matter who I worked for, I was able to say, 'Give me more,' and I'll take it on. I did a good job on each assignment, and I practically became indispensable to my boss and the organization. And here I am talking to you young folks. See, I told *my* boss I'll do that."

Best Practice

It is a best practice to ask for more. Getting your assignments or job done early, meeting all expectations is not a reflection of others' efforts or abilities but is reflective of you and your efforts. Those efforts afford you the opportunity to say, "I have completed my job and am ready for more—*give me more*."

Notes

_____

_____

_____

_____

SECTION FIVE: THE BIGGER PICTURE

* Saving to Invest
Those first paychecks may seem small (after all those deductions),
but taking advantage of some savings pays dividends, especially in
the long run.

* What's Your Plan?
Why are plans so important, and what are the ingredients of a good
plan? How do I create that plan?

* Sequencing
Setting priorities will become more and more important to you.
Allowing the right amount of time to get stuff done and putting
that stuff in a logical order will ensure you will get all done on
time. Being late is sometimes okay; early or on time is best!

* Make Visual
Using visualization techniques reduces confusion, enhances
understanding, and provides guidance and alignment. Management
by seeing is used everywhere.

* Make Accomplishments Known
The boss wants to know what his employees are doing. When you
do more than what is expected or do something outside your job
description, it is okay to let the boss know.

* Suppliers as Partners
Effectively matching customer wants to supplier wants creates
a relationship of win-win. Developing supplier *partnership style
relationships* deliver the best results.

* Those Bosses
Here we have a list of fifteen different boss types. Where does your
boss reside, and how best do you respond to that boss?

Don't save what is left after spending, but spend what is left after saving.

—Warren Buffett

When enthusiasm is inspired by reason, controlled by caution, sound in theory, practical in application, reflects confidence, spreads good cheer, raises morale, inspires associates, arouses loyalty, and laughs at adversity, it is beyond a price.

—Coleman Cox

Financial peace isn't the acquisition of stuff. It's learning to live on less than you make so you can give money back and have money to invest.

—David Ramsey

SAVING TO INVEST

Most millionaires have obtained that wealth from their parents. Others have created something special, invented a new technology or a unique gadget. Or maybe they are mostly star athletes or movie stars. Anyway, they are the ones who have the most money. These assumptions are all wrong!

Yes, they do account for a very small amount of millionaires. However, the majority of millionaires are normal, hardworking career people who...

1. live well below their means, consistently spending less than their income;
2. allocate their time, energy, and money efficiently in ways conducive to building wealth;
3. believe that financial independence is more important than displaying high social status;
4. didn't have parents who provided funding for their success;
5. have children that are economically self-sufficient;
6. are proficient in targeting marketing and business opportunities; and
7. chose the right occupation, one they like and are dedicated to (80 percent of America's millionaires are first-generation rich).[1]

Background

When you graduate and enter the workforce and earn some (your) money, you can do the things you want to do and you will now make choices as to how to spend that money. Don't be surprised or shocked by that first check or deposit! Once all the deductions are taken out, you'll see the net coming to you around 50–60 percent of the total wage.

---

[1]   Thomas J. Staley and William D. Danko, *The Millionaire Next Door*, 3–4.

One of my first bosses said, "You better save some of that money before it gets into your hands and out. Once there, it will be gone before you know it. The company does have a savings plan that automatically deducts a percentage of your wage before you ever see it. And they contribute to that savings and help you invest it. You tell them how  much to withdraw—say, 10 percent—and they'll do it for you. It's a great deal. And you'll find you really don't miss it. Do it now!"

This was some of the best advice a new wage earner could receive. Whether it is an automatic savings plan, retirement plan, or 401(k), take a good look at it, study it versus other savings options, and sign up for the one that is best for you.

If you start saving $3,000 a year (at age twenty-two), at an average rate of return of 8 percent, you will accumulate $1,070,000 by the age of sixty-five! This is based on your money contributed. If your organization or business also contributes to the investment, the wealth generated will be substantially larger.

(Albert Einstein said, "The most powerful force in the universe is compound interest.")

Best Practice

Your goal may not be to become the millionaire next door, but you will want to develop some degree of long-term financial security. Early and consistent savings with prudent investments will help you create that wealth. The earlier you start, the larger the return.

WHAT'S YOUR PLAN?

There are many plans. We have all heard of health-care plans, business plans, lesson plans, financial, marketing, production—so many plans. So what is a *real plan*? What are the key elements, and how do I create one for me or my needs?

Background

It is easy to become confused with these foundational planning terms. How do they fit? What is the correct sequence of their use?

1. Plan
2. Goals or objectives
3. Measures
4. Strategy
5. Target dates
6. Tactics

Let's switch them around and put them into sequence:

1. First is your goal or objective: What is it you want to accomplish? What is your end game or desired result?
2. Next is your strategy: What is the macro or overall method you will use to reach your goal?
3. The plan: Spell out in detail what you will do to meet your strategy and how you will measure your performance.
4. Tactics: These are the actual steps, processes, actions, or procedures you'll follow to meet your plan.
5. Measurements: Throughout the planning process, you must measure, measure your performance and progress.
6. Target dates: Target dates are desired end or completion dates. They are usually somewhat flexible but should be aggressive and realistic.

By understanding and using these six *components*, you can develop a plan and know where you are going and see if you are on or off that plan.

Example

You may decide your long-term goal is to become principal of your high school (remember, this is just an example; who would want this?).

1. My goal is to become principal. This is what I want to be. To reach this goal, I will need a long-term strategy of obtaining the education necessary to qualify.
2. My strategy is to attend a college or university, major in education or education administration, and get good grades.
3. My plan is to apply to schools that I can attend, obtain the financing to complete the required major, and obtain the grades necessary to continue the process—master's degree or PhD in education. So what are the steps (tactics) necessary to achieve this?
4. The major part of my plan revolves around the tactics I will use in my plan. These are necessary steps I must take:
   a. I need to obtain good grades that will help me get into the right schools.
   b. I need to score well on ACTs and SATs.
   c. I will need to apply to multiple schools.
   d. I will need to obtain funding.
   e. I need to develop the right curriculum that will qualify me for the job of principal.
   f. I need to obtain excellent grades to qualify me for the next steps (master's degree and then PhD.
   g. I will go to the library or other place every day to focus on my studies.
   h. Others.
5. So how am I doing? I've got my goal, my strategy, plan, and tactics. (Measuring your results at each step of the plan is critical to *making your plan*. Measuring, keeping a scorecard, and keeping your progress visible makes the plan happen. Of course, you may need to change your plan or tactics. However,

the strategy should remain constant if the actual strategy will allow you to reach your goal.)

6. Through the entire planning process, you must set target dates. By measuring and setting target dates at all times, you'll know if you are on track to meet your goal. Your first target date may be to graduate in four years. Another is to graduate with a 3.5 grade point average, preparing you for the next step.

Effectively using these six components can help you reach your goal. The next time your boss asks you, "What is your plan?" you can say, "My goal is this, strategy this, the plan and tactics are this, and I will be measuring myself against these target dates."
He will be impressed, very impressed, as you reach that goal!

Best Practice

We all have dreams, visions, aspirations, and goals.
Being very thoughtful about establishing a goal should be matched with establishing a thoughtful plan with all the components.
Without a good plan, your goal may become elusive or even unattainable.

Notes

_____

_____

_____

_____

_____

_____

_____

SEQUENCING

Sequencing means placing a priority on what needs to be done first, second, third, etc., etc., and then doing it. Sequencing is a very important part of time management—maybe the most important. It helps you decide what should be done first and last. It helps you decide what is the most important and the least.

Background

How often have you heard these:

1. "I just ran out of time, I couldn't get it all done."
2. "I had so much to do I just couldn't complete everything on time."
3. "He is always late, no matter how much he tries to be on time."

How often have you witnessed these:

1. That last-minute scramble or crash to get something done, where one would have to wing it.
2. The boss or customer standing there, waiting, waiting, waiting for something to be delivered.
3. The promise date being missed, thus disappointing someone— worst case, a customer.

Part of your job as a new worker is to manage your time and manage it so the work that is expected of you is done right and done on time. The process of *sequencing* can help you accomplish both.

Example
You are given a list of to-dos by your boss and you're expected to get them done in one shift. You have ten tasks expected to be done today and each day.

First, define and understand the ten tasks. List them in priority as to the most critical, first to be done to the last. Then assign (estimates) time needed to perform the task.

* Task 1 is the most critical and takes 30 minutes.
* Task 2 is next, 40 minutes.
* Task 3 is next, 40 minutes.
* Task 4 is next, 120 minutes.
* Tasks 5, 6, 7, 8, 9, 10 _____ minutes assigned.

By doing this, you have a game plan to do the work in a logical sequence that assures the completion of the task on time. Working your way through the tasks, you will confirm your work estimates (make adjustments) and get the work done.

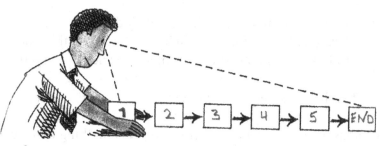

Example

Creating lists of stuff to do can also lend itself to effective sequencing. Keeping the list in front of you and marking what needs to be done first—top priority, *red*; lower priority, *yellow*; least priority (nice to dos), *green*—help you make sure the most important gets done. This color visualization of priorities works! These examples favor use of written actions to help sort and prioritize. The less-complicated, easier tasks may only require sequencing in your head. As an example, getting to work on time sure doesn't require a documented list. But if you are regularly late, maybe you should think about what needs to be done, how much time it takes, and if it is a must or want task that keeps you from being at work on time. Get the musts done, and be on time.

Best Practice

Organizing your work or tasks and putting that work in priority will help you make sure you allow enough time to complete that work in a timely fashion, allowing enough time to do a thorough, quality job. We all have time constraints that must be managed effectively. Sequencing will help do this.

Notes

_____

_____

_____

_____

_____

_____

_____

_____

_____

MAKE VISUAL

Computers, iPhones, smartphones are all great tools, tools we rely on and use every day. How can we get along without our computers or cell phones? Can't!

Another tool to help us remember, keep track, communicate, and be informed is *visualization*.

Background

I like this definition for *visualization*: "visualization is when you transform the invisible to the visible. Its purpose is to communicate data."

Every day we experience visualization; it is all around us.

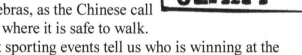

1. Speed signs tell us how fast we can legally go.
2. In a store, sales signs tell us how much we can save.
3. Crosswalks (zebras, as the Chinese call them) show us where it is safe to walk.
4. Scoreboards at sporting events tell us who is winning at the time.
5. Visual flight schedules at airports tell us where to be and when to be there.
6. Go, Stop, No Parking, Closed, Open, Men's, Ladies', and on and on are all examples of visualization.

They help us make decisions, save time, and keep us aware of what is going on.

Just as visualization is an effective tool in our everyday environment, visualization is an effective tool to use in our working experience. Here are some examples of how to use visualization in your day-to-day work:

1. Besides just talking about issues and problems, support that talking with the use of flip charts, eraser and whiteboards, anything that can communicate with pictures or data. Go beyond just talking. When we *see* information, we can better understand and remember it!

2. Identify where important items are to be (mark the area) and keep the items in those areas so you can see them and find them quickly when needed (a place for everything and everything in its place). If that area is empty it is also a visual signal.

3. Keep scores for yourself as to what *you* might want to accomplish. A personal scorecard, or scoreboard, not only keeps you aware of progress but also alerts you to changes in priorities or approaches to attain the desired score.

4. Making, using, and following up with visual lists positioned in a place you can't miss help with *forgetting*. Some leaders use legal pads.

5. Get a calendar (one that you can keep in front of you) and post the important events on that calendar.

6. What is important on your job? What is the boss expecting as results? Find a visual way to keep score on his expectations and measure your results.

7. There are always applications for visualization in your work environment that can be used for scheduling, sequencing, inventory, safety, and on and on. When all can see, all can better understand.

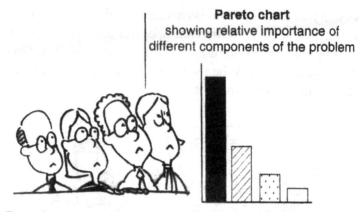

Pareto chart
showing relative importance of
different components of the problem

Best Practice

Making the invisible and complicated visible promotes better
understanding and highlights priorities. Making important
information visible helps develop the best decisions. By adding
visualization to your tool kit, your approach becomes more
balanced.

Notes

_____

_____

_____

_____

_____

_____

_____

_____

MAKE ACCOMPLISHMENTS KNOWN

Fay: "I do my job every day and a lot more. They don't even ask about the extra stuff I do, and I don't think they really see or know what I do. I figure I am here for eight-plus hours and I'll do what I think is right. Besides, I'd rather do something versus nothing. It makes the time fly, and I do have fun."

or

Alan: "I'm only going to do what they expect me to do. They only pay me for what they ask me to do, and that's all I will do. They want extra, they need to tell me what they want and pay me for it. At five, I'm outta here!"

These are two very different views of work. One is "I do and will do more than is expected, no matter if it is known or not." The other, "I am only going to do so much, unless I am paid extra to do more."

Background

Experience shows that those who draw the line (Alan) and only do so much also may be drawing the line on their advancement and potential promotion.

Fay is showing initiative and an independent, self-motivated work ethic. Fay sees work that needs to be done, has the time to do it, and does it. That initiative will be recognized and rewarded. But do others know what she is doing? Does her boss know?

Carl (the big boss) said, after a visit to look and see, "Fay, you are doing a lot of great work here, more than we are expecting. I see you have had many unforeseen and unique problems and you fixed them and kept on going. Great job! *But* nobody knows about all of what you've done and how you did it. They surely don't know about all the challenges you've faced. If others don't know about this, they'll think all is fine, the job is pretty easy, and there is nothing special going on here."

Fay: "I don't want to brag about what I have done. I feel uncomfortable about tooting my own horn. I am only doing what is needed to get the job done, whatever it takes."

Carl: "*Nonsense*, you need to tell us, report to us, and let us know all that you are doing—especially getting work done over and beyond the normal daily work. Don't try to be so humble. Do you want others here at the home office thinking you are doing nothing down there? Tell us the facts."

Best Practice

It is always a good practice to do more than what is expected—whether paid for it or not. However, when doing work over and beyond the normal, *make that work effort visible and known.* Doing more than what is expected is a good thing and should be recognized and it will be rewarded.

You are not tooting: you are enlightening!

SUPPLIERS AS PARTNERS

There are many strategies as to what is the most effective way to work with suppliers. They range from "suppliers are a dime a dozen" to "suppliers are critical to our success." Over the years, the role of the supplier has changed as organizations rely more and more on the supplier as an integral part of their total supply chain.[1]

Background

In today's world where supply chains may cross countries or even continents, the importance of suppliers has grown. That importance has grown as the global marketplace has grown. We compete where we never have before, and customers become more demanding for selection variety, for high-quality products, while expecting delivered costs to become lower and lower.
In the customer-supplier relationship, there are expectations.

Customers Want	*Suppliers Want*
Cost—the lowest price or costs. They want suppliers' prices and costs low and trending down.	*Cost*—prices that will provide the desired profit margin needed to grow the business; to be paid on time.
Quality—100 percent quality all the time, every time, with no exceptions.	*Quality*—to produce 100 percent acceptable parts.
Delivery—always on time, no misses, no backlogs, with shorter lead times.	*Delivery*—to meet schedules agreed to; longer lead times.

---

[1]   *Supply chain*—the interconnected movement of materials and information as they flow from the source to the end customer.

Continuous improvement—never-ending improvements in cost, quality, delivery, etc.

Continuous improvement—improvements that are to the benefit of both the customer and supplier.

Technology—new ideas, improvements, and breakthroughs to help the customer.

Technology—revenues or profits that allow for investments and improvements to help the customer.

Attitude—an open, honest, trustworthy relationship.

Attitude—an open, honest, trustworthy, long-term relationship.

(Note: Many of the expectations are similar, if not the same. Differences are normally open to negotiation and modified or agreed to. These negotiations, if successful, will generate a win-win agreement or contract that will provide the framework for both parties to meet their goals and objectives.)

Some customers only focus on cost, quality, and/or delivery. Depending on the product or service (office supplies, readily available consumables or services, commodities, etc.), this narrow approach may be adequate. The product or service is easy to obtain, and any failure or poor performance by the supplier is easily remedied—switch to another.

However, as suppliers become more and more critical to the success or failure of your business or organization (often accounting for 50 percent or more of *your* total cost), the customer must rely heavily on supplier performance. Any break in the supply chain can be catastrophic, and suppliers are critical to that chain's performance.

A customer who develops trust, respect, openness, honesty, and a partnering approach with key suppliers will have a propensity to be more successful. A supplier who can also develop this relationship with key customers will greatly enhance their probability of success.

Best Practice

Treating suppliers as you would want to be treated sounds logical and simple. It isn't. Problems, emergencies, and issues arise on both sides of the relationship. Being able to address those issues openly and honestly solves most problems.

Being a good supplier should be matched with being a good customer. Being able to say "You are one of my best suppliers" would only be surpassed if the supplier can say "You are my customer of choice!"

> *As I hurtled through space,*
> *one thought kept crossing my mind—*
> *every part of this rocket was supplied*
> *by the lowest bidder.*
> —Astronaut John Glenn

Suppliers are very important!

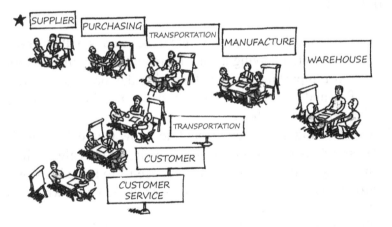

THOSE BOSSES

What should you know about your boss? What style of boss is he?
How much time should you spend with the boss? Does it make a
difference how you interact with the boss as long as you get the job
done? Is the boss always right?

Background

As your career progresses, you will have many opportunities to
learn about bosses, their techniques, their characteristics, and their
style of management. The emphasized word here is *learn*. Even
though it may seem easy to categorize the boss into one style or
another, you will find that most bosses have mixed styles and are
not dominated by one in particular.
Here are some examples of bosses you may have the opportunity to
work for, and learn from.

1. **The Pal/Buddy**. This boss wants to be friends with everyone.
   He believes that having a friendly relationship with workers is
   the most important attribute to getting the job done. He avoids
   conflict and wants to develop a personal relationship during and
   after regular work hours.
2. **The Missing**. It is often difficult to know where this boss is.
   He seems to avoid his office or work area and is always in
   'meetings/conferences/off site". He seems to leave his work
   group on automatic pilot and can seldom be found when
   decisions are needed.
3. **The Procrastinator.** In the next section of this book you will
   learn that 'facts and data will set you free'. However, this boss
   just can't move forward without more thought, preparation,
   analysis, and decision making. He seems to frequently drive up
   to, or past, deadlines. He doesn't make quick or snap decisions.
   He is very cautious.

4. **The Traditionalist**. This boss is trapped in his old practices and ideas. He would say,"If it has worked in the past, why not stick with it?" He very much values looking back at history versus looking for new approaches or ideas. He values consistency and avoids taking risks. Procedures and policies are of the utmost importance.

5. **The Workaholic.** This person is a machine. He lives for work and if he could get away with it he would be working 7 days a week. He is usually in the office first and leaves last. There is no one more dedicated than this boss. His performance is excellent, his workers respect and admire him, and he knows what is going on in the work area.

6. **The Micromanager.** This guy really gets into the details and watches very closely the output of his workers. He believes in perfection and whether it is his work or yours, he will check, and double check to insure 100% accuracy. He feels he must get into your work details just to make sure all is done correctly.

7. **The Underqualified-not Ready.** You may hear this in the work place, "how did this guy ever get the job, he doesn't know what he's doing". The new boss may fit this characterization. The new boss has a learning curve too.
More seasoned bosses may also find themselves in over their heads and need help and support.

8. **The Do it all**. Some bosses have learned through the years how to do all the jobs they are now responsible for. He feels it is easier to step in and just do what needs to be done. Getting the job done is faster, the task will be done correctly, and in some ways provides a level of security for the boss. The boss can do it all, and at times he does.

9. **The Coach**. We all love the effective coach. He shows the worker what to do, how to do it, and reinforces positive performance. The coach is a developer. He enjoys taking raw talent and molding that talent into independent, functioning workers. He enjoys teaching and values learning. The coach empowers and monitors results.

10. **The Great Boss.** This is the ideal boss. He is open, accessible, honest, trustworthy, and fair. He too sees the value of coaching and does it.

His door is always open and he creates a workplace environment that is both positive and rewarding. He empowers his workers and is available to help, when needed. This boss knows what is going on in the workplace, and engages his workers in running the business. He is open to new ideas and is willing to take some risks.

He is a good listener and his decisions are well thought out.

11. **The Innovator.** There are no boundaries to what is possible with this boss. He embraces change and newness. To him, what happened in the past is old news. Workers ideas are listened to and acted upon. He wants to get ahead and stay ahead of the competition.

    He gets bored with policies and procedures and sees them as necessary evils (at best).

12. **The Politico.** When this boss makes a move or reaches a decision first and foremost in his mind is the political impact. Doing what is right or correct takes a second position behind political considerations. His decisions will often revolve around.....

    what will my boss think

    how will this decision impact my career,

    and will my decision be seen as a positive or negative decision?

    The Politico makes decisions based upon the me, not the we.

13. **The Bean Counter.** Everything is about the numbers. This boss believes in measurement and tracking performance at every step. The human side of the work environment comes in second to the financials. Costs, cost savings and expenditure control are the major areas of focus. Creating a budget and sticking to it is paramount.

14. **The Unprepared.** Some bosses just can't help themselves. They do not do their homework or prepare for that next meeting or that next day. They tend to be quick on their feet and often are seen as 'winging it'. Practice and preparation are not important to them.

15. **The Antagonist.** Most bosses attempt to have their groups work together. Teamwork and supportive participation are their approach. The antagonist is different. He promotes

discord between workers in an attempt and belief that conflict will create energy, develop enthusiasm, and generate open discussion that will more effectively solve problems. Conflict and stress are his tools to precipitate confrontation, participation, and progress. Creating an antagonistic, competitive environment is his goal.

Luckily or unluckily, I have not had the opportunity to work for all fifteen types of bosses. However, there are five that are somewhat common, and I may have learned something of value that will help you with adapting to their style:

1. *Workaholic*
   Of course, there is a lot to admire when the boss is a workaholic. However, most of us want to focus on our job, meet or exceed the boss's expectations, and do what is needed to be successful—and have a life. The best recommendation here is to be very clear on what the boss's expectations are, and for you and the boss to have a shared understanding of those expectations. It is important for the boss to know (reviews, reports, meetings, e-mails) you are focused on the work and you are getting it done. Absolutely do not become a clock-watcher. Quitting time is making sure all is covered for the day and you are well lined up for the next day. As I noted in practice 1, *in early out late* shows your dedication to the work without being a workaholic.

2. *Traditionalist*
   The traditionalist will expect you to do your work, as it has been done, to procedures, to process, or to policy. That is what he expects, and you should work hard to comply to them. As you obtain additional experience and find a more efficient way to do the work, take this new idea to the boss as an improvement or enhancement to the current procedure. Explain the benefits and show how you've considered any negatives to the change. With a thoughtful, well-analyzed improvement proposition, the boss may take a chance on it. He will be cautious and have to think about it. That's okay.

If that suggestion is accepted and works, your boss will be more receptive to change ideas when coming from you. If that suggestion is accepted and it fails, you will have a more difficult time getting the boss to listen to change ideas.

3. *Micromanager*

Usually, a micromanager is concerned with perfection and having no errors. Of course, he has more experience than you and may be better trained in this work. The best approach is to make sure your work is of the highest quality and has no errors. Each time the micromanager finds something (and they will search for that something) with errors, it will reinforce his need to check on you and your work. Therefore, check and double-check your work. Also, let the boss know that he should feel comfortable with the minor stuff you do (you always check it 100 percent) and you look forward to learning more about the more complicated work he does.

Remember, do not take micromanaging of your work as personal. The micromanager does this with his other people.

4. *Underqualified*

Whether you're a boss or a worker, there will be times (as you move up) you too might be considered underqualified. The underqualified can be a good boss, and the best approach is to help the boss be successful. What you bring to the job can help the boss better understand the work and make him more and more qualified. This assistance or partnering will not be forgotten by the boss. Many feel that their job is to make the boss a success, to never let him fail. Not a bad idea!

5. *Great*

This is the boss we all want—the listener, the team builder, the coach, the boss that motivates the entire group to excel. He creates a work environment that is task oriented, recognizes success, and promotes having some fun on the job. With this boss you should take notes and document all the approaches and practices he uses that makes him a great boss. Those that you can apply to your work area, do so. Practice what you are learning from this boss and make those practices yours.

Sounds like this is what this book is all about.

Best Practice

You will have many bosses, and learning about and understanding these bosses will help you in meeting your work objectives. The five I selected were the ones that, more likely than not, you will experience. To be the most effective in understanding and managing your boss,

1. try to understand your boss's style of management and work within that style—spend a fair amount of time to watch and learn his style;
2. focus on your work and its objectives—no matter the style of the boss, there is always a way to succeed under his management, and doing what is expected 100 percent of the time will make you successful; Knowing what the boss expects and wants is very important
3. find better or smarter ways to do your work as this will be accepted by all bosses—some acceptance comes faster, some slower; and
4. remember, you can learn from anyone—take note of the habits of the boss you've liked and not liked.

SECTION SIX: THE NEXT LEVEL

* Continuous Improvement Beats Postponed Perfection
This is a long title to say making incremental improvements (step/step) usually delivers the best results as you learn and grow. It usually beats waiting, waiting, waiting for undelivered perfection.

* Facts and Data Will Set You Free
What is a sound process for making those decisions before you? When do you draw the line and make the decision and go for it?

* Compartmentalization
This is a technique to help you manage many tasks and allow you to complete them one by one as needed. Get those drawers ready.

* Customers Rule
Customers are people; most are nice and reasonable, while others will challenge your patience and endurance. Is the customer always right? The customer does pay you.

* People Make the Difference
In most cases, we can all buy the same materials, buy the same machinery or tools, install the same methods or procedures. What makes the difference of how everything works are the people.

* Attitude Feeds All
There is nothing more important to attaining success than displaying a good and positive attitude. This is the *best* of the best practices.

Excellent firms don't believe in excellence—only in constant improvement and constant change.

—Tom Peters

There is little difference in people, but that little difference makes a big difference. The little difference is attitude. The big difference is whether it is positive or negative.

—W. Clement Stone

When you choose to be pleasant and positive in the way you treat others, you have also chosen, in most cases, how you are going to be treated by others.

—Zig Ziglar

Do more than belong: participate!
Do more than care: help!
Do more than believe: practice!
Do more than be fair: be kind!
Do more than forgive: forget!
Do more than dream: work!

—William Arthur Ward

CONTINUOUS IMPROVEMENT BEATS
POSTPONED PERFECTION

Change is rather uncomfortable for some people (maybe even most people). We all get into routines, into comfort zones, and when someone or something rocks the boat, we have a tendency to recoil or even push back on that change. Real change is seldom easy. Most people do not resist change; they resist being changed.

One of America's most successful business leaders, Lee Iococca, said this about change: "We are in serious trouble, and we are going to make change, and that means we are going to take risks. I need all of you on board. I expect you to *lead, follow, or get out of the way.*"

He is rather blunt about his view of change. It is needed and coming, and the choices of roles are spelled out.

Background

The successful organizations that I have been affiliated with promote and actually embrace change as a way to grow and flourish. If you don't change, don't make improvements these organizations recognize, you just won't survive.

As you start that new job, at first you'll just want to survive at getting the job done. What to do, when to do it, and to make sure what you do is right are the first priorities. However, shortly you'll have that job down pat and will realize, *I can do this better if I make such in such a change.*

Making *incremental improvements* to your job, to your process, allows you to...

1. get the job done faster,
2. get the job done with less labor,
3. improve the quality of your work,
4. improve your accuracy,
5. get more efficient,
6. probably reduce costs,
7. have more fun and get a little creative, and
8. maybe go back to your boss and say, "I've got that job done with some improvements. What more can I do?" (The boss likes improvements and values someone wanting to do more.)

Once you get into the habit of looking for improvements and making those improvements work for you, you'll find that change is not so uncomfortable or threatening. Change becomes a way of life, the norm, and comfortable. It becomes an opportunity for you to be a leader in support of your organization's success.

Many organizations employ various improvement or change processes. They do this to survive and stay alive in their competitive marketplace. Six Sigma, Kaizen, Lean Manufacturing, TQM, Baldrige Performance Excellence are but a few of them. Their goal is to incrementally improve the organization, not just talk, think, or procrastinate about improvement (postponed perfection).

Continuous Improvement
Change!!

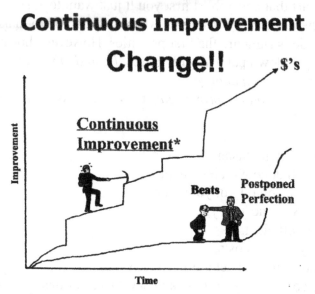

One extremely successful manufacturing plant came up with a JDIT program—just do it. All employees were trained in the program, and each person was expected to participate at making improvements and helping the organization's survival. The organization did survive and it has flourished!

Best Practice

By incorporating in your thought processes and then your actual implementation a mind-set of incremental continuous improvement, you can instill this best practice. Some can do this, some not.

If you can, you will have a major advantage over *your* competition.

Notes

_____

_____

_____

FACTS AND DATA WILL SET YOU FREE

In walks our new boss, all smiles and ready to soothe everyone
about the current job situation. It was bleak; that's why so many
lost their jobs. The boss started by saying how unfortunate it was
for those who did lose their jobs. He said, "We must do better,
or we too will lose our jobs. It's nothing personal, just business."
Hmmmmm, not personal?
That sure soothed everyone!
Then after about an hour of reviewing the situation, the boss
said, "We will succeed as long as we work together, focus on our
customers, and when we make decisions they will be thoughtful
and fact driven. *Facts and data will set you free.*"
I turned to the guy next to me and said, "I wonder what that
means?" Soon I learned!

Background

Every day we are afforded the opportunity to make decisions. Many
of these decisions are almost automatic. We aren't required to spend
a lot of time or energy to make them. And since many aren't all that
important or critical, we make them and get on with it.

1. What do I need to do first
   today?
2. What am I going to wear to
   work today?
3. What meetings are scheduled
   for today? Do I attend all of
   them?
4. Where are we going for lunch?
5. What time do we meet after work?

These decisions are somewhat important, but if made incorrectly, there is probably little or no consequence as a result of them. And they can be remedied relatively easily.

This now leads us to *facts and data will set you free.* What does it mean?

As we attempt to make more important decisions, we are often faced with "Is this the right decision or not? I keep thinking about it, but I'm not sure. How can I be sure? Others are counting on me? Should I ask others what they think? How long do I wait?"

The more critical the decision, the more data you need to gather. Asking questions of others and doing some homework is a good start. Write down what you hear and learn.

Any and all sources are good. Try to sort through the information you've gathered and evaluate the following:

1. Is what I gathered true?
2. Is the source reliable?
3. How can I confirm what is correct?
4. What have others done in the past, and how did that turn out?
5. What does my boss think of what I've learned?
6. What are my ideas? What are the ideas of the others?
7. Do I have enough resources, data, inputs, and even opinions?

There is a lot to factor into making good decisions. Here are seven basic steps to help you through this process:

1. Before doing anything, *stop* other tasks, slow down, and focus on this decision.
2. Establish the goal of the decision. What do you want to accomplish? What is your desired deliverable?
3. Bring forth all those facts, data, inputs, and opinions you've gathered; study them.
4. Develop options that *could* meet your goal; there should be numerous potential options.

5. For each option, consider the consequences of implementing that option. What are the potential results, good and bad?
6. Choose what you believe is the best option. This option attains your goal. This option has the best probability of success. Implement this best option.
    a. Set yourself free!
7. Watch and monitor your results. If modifications are needed, make changes.

You should now feel comfortable; you've done your homework, looked at all the data, analyzed the facts. You've made that decision; therefore, you are free. The decision is made based on best information and evidence at that point in time.

Best Practice

By doing your homework, gathering data, then analyzing that data (verifying the facts) and making a decision, you can now feel comfortable. Remember at that decision time, you've made the best decision, a decision based on what you know. Therefore, facts and data did set you free!

Notes

_____

_____

_____

_____

_____

_____

_____

COMPARTMENTALIZATION

One of your work challenges will be keeping all those balls in the air that seem to come your way. Or another way to say it, "getting a lot of pots on the fire and trying to keep them from boiling over." So how do you deal with the pressure—people, workload, family, projects, social life, home—all at once? *You don't!*

Background

There is a technique called compartmentalization. Some people are born with this capability and really don't know it. Others learn it, apply it, drastically reduce their job pressure and obtain excellent results. It does require discipline, self-training, and focus. Here is how compartmentalization works: *in your mind and/or in your workplace environment you learn to segregate, isolate, focus, and complete the task.*

You often hear, "You can't let your personal life spill over into your work. You have to keep them separate, and you don't want either of them affecting the other." At least that is the goal. Compartmentalization takes this illustration to the next step and has you organize your projects (for lack of a better term) into freestanding, distinct items that do not spill over and that allows you to focus on that one project when you want to or need to. Think of it this way: each project gets a drawer in a chest of drawers that holds that and only that project.

When you need to work on that project, you pull out that drawer, focus on that project, and when time is up, close that drawer and go to the next project.

This allows you to isolate multiple areas, focus on that area when needed, and put it away when not needed.

Here are some steps to get started:

1. Select a focus—isolated it away (drawer) from all other issues you might deal with.
2. Select other focus topics.
   (There might be 4-8 areas (drawers) deserving focus -your call on the number)
3. When you open that drawer, apply extreme focus and work on that topic. That focus should be for a relatively short time to make progress, not necessarily complete the project. When finished, close the drawer.
4. Move forward through the drawers in slow, regular steps— maybe make sure you open each one daily and always keep an eye on the project target completion date or promise date.
5. When working in that drawer, don't beat that project to death— remember to think step by step as you move toward that completion date. Open the drawer, do the work, close it, and move on.
6. If you designate eight drawers, hold the line and say no to adding more till one of the eight is empty. Then fill it, if you need.

This systematic separation approach has many advantages:

1. You set your priorities—you organize and segregate them.
2. You become more focused, pay better attention to detail.
3. You won't jump from one topic to another; you won't shift gears unnecessarily.
4. You will get more done.
5. Boredom of staying on one project too long is eliminated.
6. Quality of your product will be improved.
7. You will regularly *see* and meet target dates more effectively.
8. Your actual output and productivity increases.

9. Compartmentalization runs counter to multitasking. There is a place for each. But what compartmentalization does is require focus, focus, focus!

Best Practice

Compartmentalize when you need to segregate and focus on multiple topics or projects. Compartmentalization will reduce spillover, task interference, workplace disruption and reduce stress!

Notes

_____

_____

_____

_____

_____

_____

CUSTOMERS RULE

"That guy is a real jerk. He comes in here every day, never says hello, thank you, or anything. He's a real grump."

"Do you think she would have her money out when the bill is totaled—with a long line waiting on her. Oh no, she finally opens her purse, searches for her wallet, gets out her money, and counts out to the penny the exact amount. Did she think the stuff was free?"

"I have to say, *may I help you and thank you*, so I do. Who cares!"

"That meeting with the customer was terrible. He told us what he wanted and didn't care how we got it done. If we don't get the problem fixed, he said we're out!"

"Who does she think she is? Her requests are unreasonable and can't be met. She'll find that out when she doesn't get it filled!"

So how is your day going?

Background

These few examples do reflect some of the frustration when dealing directly with customers. Whether you are dealing with customers in the open marketplace, in meetings, or engaging them across the negotiating table, you will learn one fact.

Customers are very unique. They are people, and no two are alike. Some are easy to deal with, some not. Some are engaging, some not. One customer will say, "How are you, and thank you," and mean it. On the other end, the customer will say nothing and mean it. Some will treat you with utmost respect, and others will almost ignore you.

As a new worker, having the opportunity to participate with customers, you need to be professional, confident, and non-combative. The best approach is to use the customer contact opportunity while harboring no preconceived ideas or opinions.

Customers are diverse, and so are servers and suppliers (like you). How a customer responds can be directly attributable to how the server or supplier responds.

1. Is the customer always right? If he isn't, should I avoid telling him?
2. Can a customer be insulting and get away with it?
3. Do I need to always be at the customer's beck and call?
4. Do I tell the customer what he wants to hear? Do I lie?
5. Do I shield the customer from the truth?
6. Are customers always unreasonable?

The answers are no, no, no, no, no, and no.
First we need to establish the basic concept of who pays. As Henry Ford said, "It is not the employer who pays the wages. Employers only handle the money. It is the *customer* who pays the wages." With no customers, there is no revenue; no revenue means no wages, and no wages means no job! Very simple, very direct, and very real. Therefore, with all the challenges you may face dealing with customers, the reality is the customer pays *you*!
What should a new worker keep in mind when dealing with customers? What are sound basic principles of being customer led?

1. First, recognize all customers are not the same. Treat each as an individual and treat each professionally and with respect.
2. Get to know your customers. In some cases, actually study them, their business, their goals and objectives. The more you know about your customer, the better. Getting into the shoes of your customer may help you get into step with his needs and challenges. You can learn a lot about customers outside the day-to-day work area. Invest the time to do this.
3. Listen to your customers. Customers want to be heard, be understood, and know that you are listening. Keep notes and document the customer's key points. Any customer insult should be ignored or at best categorized as "unintended poor choice of words."
4. Ask questions. Make sure you are clear as to customer expectations. The clearer they are with you, the better chance you have of meeting those expectations.

5. Be honest with the customer. Good news is easy to convey. Bad news is just plain uncomfortable. Just the same, the customer will appreciate the truth, especially when he knows you are telling him about the real situation.
6. Keep yourself calm. Unreasonably demanding customers will not be neutralized with anger or aggressive responses. Sometimes those unreasonable demands, once fully understood and analyzed, are not only not unreasonable but quite doable.
7. Prepare for the meeting with the customer. You do represent your company or organization. The customer will value seeing his supplier team as knowledgeable, focused, and responsive. Be prepared to be very responsive to the customer's needs. "Does he expect me to turn on a dime?" (*Yes.*)
8. Being humble won't hurt. There will be times you will be more knowledgeable or more up-to-date than the customer. How you effectively convey that information to the customer will be important to the relationship.
9. Make recommendations to help the customer. Your ideas, if well thought out and based on learning, experience, and data, will be well received.
10. Last, always follow up. Any assignments made or expectations established with the customer should be captured, documented, and acted upon so the customer knows you are working for him. Never, never allow customer follow-up assignments fall into that *black hole*!

Now, back to those no, no, no, no, no, and nos. The ten principles listed address these no's and more. Customer satisfaction is a key underpinning of supplier success. It takes understanding, work, dedication, and commitment.

Best Practice

Understanding that you are paid by the customer and making that customer successful makes you successful. This is universally recognized and accepted—no customer, no job, no pay. When you have the opportunity to interact with a customer, make it a positive one for the customer and yourself. Your pay may depend upon it.

Positive Customer Satisfaction Comes in Many Forms
A few years ago, our family went to a small mom-and-pop
restaurant for breakfast. There were but ten tables and one busy
waitress. After we surveyed the menu, the waitress approached and
just stood there, not saying a word, awaiting someone to start the
orders. My brother-in-law said, "I'll take number 2—the traditional
breakfast." My wife said, "Number 4, the waffles." All of us
followed. Last to place the order was my sister, and she said, "I
don't see what I'm looking for, so I'll take 3, pancakes."
The waitress stopped writing, looked at my sister, and finally said
her first words, "No, you don't!"
In shock, my sister looked up at the waitress and stumbled with
"I-I-I just wanted three pancakes."
"*No, you don't!* You won't be able to eat them. Each pancake is
larger than the plate, and no one eats three. You want one."
"Yes," my sister said, "I want one!"
My sister barely finished the *one* pancake. She was delighted by
the food and the unique method used by the waitress to help the
customer not make a mistake.

* * *

A young man was selling frozen ice cream, soft drinks, and
popsicles as he walked by the hundreds of people on the hot New
Jersey beach. As he strolled from blanket to blanket, umbrella to
umbrella, his attention-getting phrase was "Ice cream, ice cream.
The best in town, cold, and refreshing," and with a *big smile* on his
face, he yelled out, "Give your chick a lick a on a stick, give your
tongue a sleigh ride. I'm your man with a plan, stay cool getting
that tan."
Even those who really didn't initially want an ice cream bought one
because of the unique pitch.

* * *

Customers are important; they pay you!

PEOPLE MAKE THE DIFFERENCE

In most businesses or organizations, four basic groups are expected to be in alignment and perform effectively:

Man, material, methods, and machinery

Toyota's basic principle is to develop these groups to work in harmony and balance. This best practice focuses on *man*.

Background

Whether you are in business, education, government, or another field, all four of these groups (M-M-M-M) are available.
With the right selection and adequate funding,

1. we can all buy the same materials,
2. we can all buy the same machinery, and
3. in most cases, we can all buy or develop (benchmark) the same methods.

Man is different—*unique*. Man is the integrator of the other three. Man can adjust to changing circumstances. Man can adjust the machines, the material, and of course, the method. Man can adapt.

Therefore, man is the special group. *People make the difference.*

Most organizations attempt to recruit people that

1. have a positive attitude;
2. can adapt to and even promote positive change;
3. work hard, aggressively, with speed;
4. are engagers and doers, are action oriented;
5. are willing to listen, learn, and grow on the job; and
6. are team players who value and respect others.

Most organizations continually *invest* in their people by

1. providing regular on-the-job training;
2. sending their people for further formal education;
3. sending their people to training session, seminars, and conferences; and
4. providing job rotation and expanded experience and opportunity.

Man, the human resource, plays the most important role in the long-term success and viability of any organization. Investment in the human resource consistently delivers the best results.

Best Practice

Learning to effectively work with others, whether you are a follower or a leader, is a key because *people make the difference.*

In organizations, small or large, the key ingredient to success is the people.

Alaska Airlines[2]
Advertisement in the *Wall Street Journal*, May 17, 2014
"Alaska Airlines Awarded Highest in Customer Satisfaction Among Traditional Carriers in North America by J. D. Power Seven Years in a row."

"It's our employees who make the difference."

Man is recognized here as the success factor; people made *the difference!*

---

2   At Alaska Airlines they have the following:

Machine—uses Boeing 737s available to all airlines.

Materials—uses standard jet fuel, oils, lubricants available to all airlines.

Methods—uses the same basic FAA guidelines and other operation methods followed by all airlines.

ATTITUDE FEEDS ALL

I have saved the most important practice for last. All the best practices explained in this book are important, and their collective use will greatly enhance your ability to be successful. Some of these practices you may already use, while others need to be thought through, understood, practiced, and made part of your day-to-day routine.

Attitude stands on its own and permeates each of the other forty-nine practices. How often have you heard "Boy, she sure has a great attitude" or "Don't have such a bad attitude, look at the bright side"? It is your choice to be made; promote a good or positive attitude that can help you be successful, or accept a neutral or negative attitude that (at best) doesn't help you.

Background

How do you define a positive attitude? What differentiates a positive attitude from a neutral attitude or even from a bad attitude? Some common definitions of a positive attitude are as follows:

* Those displaying a disposition of optimism and encouragement.
* Those individuals that possess a glass full versus half-empty mentality.
* Those who don't ignore problems when they crop up. Instead, they face the problems head on and do something productive to change the outcome.
* Those who speak of the positives and avoid speaking of negatives.
* Those who readily say "Good morning," "How are you," and "Good evening" and mean it!

So on this last best practice, you have an opportunity for a short quiz as to what attitude you possess. Be honest because this quiz is to help you.

Yes = 2, Sometimes = 1, Seldom or Never = 0

1. When something doesn't go your way, do you accept that disappointment and move forward? Do you look at why this happened and try to figure out how to avoid this disappointment in the future?
2. As you come across coworkers, customers, even those you don't know, do you look them in the eye and smile? Are you friendly?
3. When your group or team loses, do you have a tendency to try to lift them up and help them move forward?
4. Are you happy with others' successes even when you don't benefit from that success?
5. When others succeed, do you enjoy saying "Great job," "Congratulations," and "Let's celebrate"?
6. Do you focus on the future and looking forward versus the past and looking backward? Are your best days still ahead of you?
7. Do you avoid gossip and joining in or agreeing with negative talking about coworkers or the boss?
8. Do you avoid negative people?
9. Do you address problems when they come up and avoid delaying action?
10. Do you listen to others' point of view and value their inputs?

Most graduates will see their score somewhere in the middle 10–15 from a maximum of 20. Those areas where you give yourself a 0 are opportunities to improve your attitude portfolio.

Since attitude is so important and a major underpinning of the forty-nine practices, here are some suggestions that will help you and help you create an environment of positive attitudes:

1. Remember, you create your attitude, no one else does. What is handed to you and how you respond is the basis of your attitude. No excuses. Your attitude is yours. Take charge of it.
2. Face failure and disappointment as the normal part of life. There are always winners and losers.

Failure is simply the opportunity to begin again, this time more intelligently.

—Henry Ford

Success is a lousy teacher. It seduces smart people into thinking they can't lose.

—Bill Gates

It is fine to celebrate success, but it is more important to heed the lessons of failure.

—Bill Gates

3. With all the negatives around us, find or search out the positive. Frowns are often met with frowns, smiles with smiles. You will be surprised how smiling and laughing uplifts others and yourself.

4. Avoid angry, negative people. Don't let their attitudes spill upon and affect you. Don't waste your time trying to change their attitudes; focus on yourself. Associate with others that are positive.
5. Language plays an important part in attitude:

   a. Avoid: "I can't, impossible, no way, won't work, never, always."

   b. Promote: "I think I can do that, that's possible, that could work, sometimes, usually."

How do you respond when someone asks, "How are you?"
a. Avoid: "Okay, hangin' there, not bad, tolerable."
b. Promote: "Terrific, fantastic, couldn't be better."

6. Allocate time for yourself to step out of the daily race and have a few laughs with coworkers or even the boss. Laughing is contagious. As I said in practice number 9, you are allowed to have fun at work.
7. Look for good, positive qualities in others; appreciate them, understand them, and see if they can apply to you.
8. Slow down and think twice and act once. You are not expected to make snap judgments. Mistakes will be minimized, your performance enhanced.
9. Do some pre work exercise; listen to some uplifting music and try to get fired up for work and seeing your friends there. Think of something positive or fun for the day. Don't show up half-asleep.

Best Practice

Having a positive, can-do attitude not only will serve you in the workplace but will also become contagious and help create a positive attitude within your group.

The longer I live, the more I realize the impact of attitude on life. Attitude, to me, is more important than the past, than education, than money, than circumstances, than failures, than successes, than what other people think, say, or do. It is more important than appearances, giftedness, or skill. It will make or break a company, a church, a home. The remarkable thing is we have a choice every day regarding the attitude we embrace for that day. We cannot change our past, we cannot change the fact that people will act in a certain way. We cannot change the inevitable.

*The one thing we can do is play on the one string we have, and that is our attitude. **I am convinced that life is 10% what happens to me and 90% how I react to it.** And so is it with you.*

We are in charge of our attitudes.
—Charles R. Swindoll

Today will be the ***best day ever!***
If you can start each day with this short phrase, you are off to a great start with a positive attitude! Others will see it, appreciate it, and will want to join in.

Notes

_____

_____

_____

_____

_____

_____

_____

_____

_____

_____

_____

THE END
IS REALLY THE BEGINNING

Now that you have read the fifty practices, the next steps are up to you. As I said at the beginning of this book, these practices have been gleaned from and improved upon from some very successful people. Today you have an opportunity to take advantage of their skills and learning.

As a high school graduate, advanced education graduate, or military service person who is transitioning into the day-to-day civilian workforce, you now have before you some of the best approaches that will help you develop your career. You will find some of these are easy to implement, some more difficult. The speed by which you can adopt these practices is up to you. However, the sooner you start implementation, the better. And as said before, consistency is very important.

One of the best practice contributors recently said, "I wish I had known all of this when I was in my twenties. I could have saved a lot of time. Some of it was just wasted time."

A recent Purdue graduate spoke of what she learned in a very short time as she entered the competitive workforce. Not surprising, her findings are very consistent with the *Graduate Handbook:*

1. Be nice and ask others for help.
2. Work harder than you need to work.
3. Success runs parallel to happiness.
4. You are not entitled.
5. Enjoy what you are doing and do it well.
6. You are not as busy as you think.
7. My new priority:
   a. Customer first
   b. Company second

   c. Business third
   d. Organization fourth
   e. Me last

At the start of this book, we discussed what *success* is. You need to decide what success is for *you*. What you decide today may differ in the future. However, remember, what you decide is your decision.

Today, if someone asks me what I need to do to be successful, I can say read *The Graduate Handbook*. It will surely help you!

With use of *The Graduate Handbook*, your probability of success will increase, reaching your goals will be accelerated, and truly you will have more fun as you travel that road.

I wish you the best as you start that new work experience.

Now you do know some of what you didn't know.

And, remember,

"When the sun comes up, you better be running!"

—Russell J. Bunio

ACKNOWLEDGMENT

I wish to thank all of you who have helped and guided me through this book. I am very grateful for the time, effort, and inputs you provided:

Brain Appleyard
Mary Bunio
Connie Bunio
Suzanne Cannon
Jackson Cannon
Cindy Code
Pepper Deschantel
Ralph Holroyd
Thomas Hoag
Laura Lightstone
Larisa Lightstone
Emily Myers
Jamie Snydel
Nancy Drinkhall Snyder

I also want to acknowledge and thank Oriel Stat a Matrix for permitting me to use drawings from the book *The Team Handbook, Third Edition* (www.teamhandbook.com). Reprinted with permission.

SOURCES OF BEST PRACTICES

Bosses

Charles Terry ....Foreman, GM
Galen Myers.......................General Foreman, GM
Hap Grieshop ....Superintendent, GM
Ron Vonderheide ....Administrator, GM
Carl Code ....Director, Materials Management, GM
Gary Woodall....................Plant Manager, GM Mexico
Robert Schuler ....Plant Manager, GM Mexico
S. Uchikawa ....General Manager, NUMMI (GM and Toyota JV)
H. Kinoshita......................General Manager, NUMMI (GM and Toyota JV)
Mark Chesnut....................VP, Human Resources, Cummins Engine Co.
James Henderson ....Chairman, Cummins Engine Co.
Joseph Loughrey................Executive Vice President, Cummins Engine Co.
Tim Solso ....President, Cummins Engine Co.[1]
Alan Mulally.....................President, BCAG, The Boeing Co.[2]

Coworkers

Ron DeCarlo ....Purchasing Manager, GM
Joseph Schrantz ....Manager, GM Mexico
Dave Cairoli......................Manager, GM Mexico
Preston Crabill ....Manager, GM Mexico

Employees

Rodney O'Neal ....General Motors Institute, Student in Training[3]
Ted Agata..........................Manager NUMMI Office, Detroit[4]
Larry Husmann..................Director of Purchasing, Cummins Engine Co.
Hope Cantrell....................Director of Materials, Cummins Engine Co.

---

[1]   Present Chairman of the Board of General Motors Corporation.

[2]   President of the Ford Motor Co. (retired 2014).

[3]   CEO Delphi Automotive, PLC. (Retired 2015)

[4]   Present Vice President Toyota Motor Co.

Kathy Banks ....Director of Quality, Cummins Engine Co.

Rebecca Swift...................Administrative Assistant, Cummins Engine Co.

Eldon McBride..................Director, Human Resources, The Boeing Co.

Associates

Lee Cutrone ....President and CEO, Trustmark Bank, Houston, Texas

Don Snydel........................VP, Creative Printing Services

Les Andersen.....................VP, Human Resources, Longs Drug Stores

Anthony Torcasio..............Vice Chairman, The May Department Stores Company

Robert Rohrbaugh ....Chief Prosecutor, State of Maryland

Ren Bing Bing ....Vice President, Supply Management, Weichai Power Co.

Cheng Huiming.................Manager of Technical Department, Weichai Power Co.

Carmen Castillo................President, Superior Design International

Steve Broback ....Thunder Lizard Productions and Parnassus Group

William Biel......................VP, Merrill Lynch

Harriet Michel...................President, National Minority Supplier Development Council

NOTES

NOTES

NOTES

NOTES

NOTES

NOTES

NOTES

NOTES